e
pa

volume 1

black dog
publishing
london uk

Introduction
Dalibor Vesely

In introducing the work of a creative practice there is a temptation to situate the work in 'a particular category', to speak about received influences and even about a style of the practice. However this ambition is today not only difficult, but virtually impossible to fulfil. We have moved a long way from the relative comfort of the last century avant-gardes, from movements and groups supported by their programmes and manifestos. Our own era is characterised by splintered identities, competing ideologies, fractured parties and aggressive self-presentation of competing practices and businesses.

It is rather typical that architects are more aware of the differences that separate them and give to their work an aura of novelty and originality, leaving behind the common references and goals which contribute to the long term cultural references and goals which contribute to the long term cultural relevance of their work. This emphasis on differences and originality leads not only to the questionable merits of the results, but also to an isolation from the latent world of culture, which we all, in one way or another, share.

The fragmented nature of contemporary culture obscures, most of all, the fact that behind visible appearances there are levels of reality we cannot fully control, and yet they determine the nature of our history. On these, deeper levels of reality we encounter tendencies of surprising universality and unifying power. The most obvious is the overwhelming power of technology, seen not only as a human invention but as a historical destiny. The technical homogenisation of modern life makes it much easier to share the illusion that even the most abstract architectural solutions, based on narrow technical criteria, may be adequate and appropriate. Human adaptability is an important factor in the cultivation of this illusion. However, even more important is the overwhelming and persuasive role of emancipated representation, in which only the levels of reality expressed in technical language are addressed. It is extraordinary how many different forms and faces this language can adopt. And yet, behind all the faces, there is a common set of characteristics that we can find not only in the areas normally associated with production and technology but also with the field of creative activity. The monologue of the technologically oriented design of high-tech architecture or of so called "intelligent buildings" has reached the level of controlled operations in virtual space and the field described most recently as an architecture of "telepresence". Telepresence is a transformation of the traditional fabric of architecture, including our own corporeal involvement into a 'new' reality structured by electronic media.

The anonymity and the disembodied nature of modern technology is complemented by a second main modern tendency, represented by an introverted and highly personalised culture. It is a sign of the avant-garde mentality that the architect sees himself as a sole agent, fully responsible for everything related to creativity. This illusion culminates in the belief that the world is essentially his own world. The concentration on private experience, imagination and fantasy contradicts the very nature of architecture, which is always open to and judged by a shared public culture.

The distance and the loose link between the culture of personal experience and the sphere of the shared, but very abstract culture, which is dominated by instrumental thinking, can be described as the "grey zone of modernity". The grey zone is a source of unprecedented freedom to produce, but is also a source of an overwhelming relativism, loss of meaning, narrowing down of the sphere of reference and as a result, of a general cultural malaise. The nature of this malaise can be best illustrated by the dilemma facing most contemporary architects. On one hand it is assumed that true creative architecture should be free of all historical and other unnecessary cultural references, in order to be as original and unique as possible, and at the same time it is expected that the result should be understood, appreciated and accepted universally. This dilemma can be sustained only by a self-centred culture, prepared to share the dilemma as a norm.

The work of Eric Parry Architects (EPA) is situated deliberately in the "grey zone of modernity". The choice is motivated by an awareness that the gap between personal experience and instrumental culture, if it is recognised as a problem, reveals the presence of a latent culture, which can serve as a foundation for a different kind of design. The term "latent culture" is an attempt to describe the silent background of everyday reality. The term is a result of recent investigations into the pre-reflective levels of reality, which show that the pre-reflective world is not amorphous or chaotic, but well structured, with a clear sense of meaning, and unity. What latent culture lacks is explicit articulation and thus the possibility of being readily shared, which does not mean that it is only personal or subjective. In fact the opposite is the case. Because it is constituted spontaneously in a direct response to the natural conditions mediated by cultural tradition, the latent culture is the primary source and measure of objectivity. The objectivity of latent culture is most clearly manifested in typical human situations, such as different types of work, reading, listening to music, dining etc..

Typical situations represent the most complete way of understanding not only the nature of particular events but also the corresponding experience of the surrounding world and the human qualities of the world. Typical situations endow experience with durability in relation to which other experiences can acquire meaning and can form a memory and history. They also explain the relationship between the cultural conditions, memories, expectations, visible physiognomy of the space and the spatial structure of a particular situation. The work of EPA, based on these principles, can be described as a situational approach to design. This approach is not a direct reference to the forgotten latent world. It is rather a thoughtful attempt to situate the instrumental culture with all its technological

possibilities in the broader and deeper horizon of the latent world. A good example of this is the office building at Stockley Park near Heathrow Airport. This building takes advantage of being situated at the edge of the newly created lake. In the original proposal the lake was connected with the atrium in the heart of the building by a channel of water parallel with the axis of the entry through the vestibule. The channel of water is complemented by a skylight of the same size and orientation above it. The link between the channel and the skylight creates a cut through the first floor. The nature and the arrangement of the space on the first floor is particularly characteristic of the thinking of Eric Parry and his team. The character of the open plan office space is defined by the translucent glass block walls and continuous, narrow ribbon windows. The contrast between the semi-transparency of the walls and the full transparency of the windows creates a strong sense of horizon and engagement of the building with its surroundings. To appreciate the engaging and integral role of the horizon, we have to pause and reflect on experience, which may appear in the middle of a busy day as too obvious if not banal.

The deeper meaning of horizon has its origin in the experience of the imaginary line where the earth meets the sky. The nature of this imaginary horizontal line is revealed in its power to define the boundary of our visible world, as well as in the invitation to transcend this boundary. The association of the horizon with the surface of the earth is a deeply rooted measure for everything that is above and below, far and near. It is not surprising that the concept of 'horizon' played a decisive role in the formation of our language, our thinking and our world. By defining the limits of visibility, receding with our movement, but not disappearing, the horizon became an integrating vehicle of reference and continuity for everything in the visible world. Because the horizon belongs to the human way of seeing the world, it is a decisive aspect of the human situation in that it holds it together and gives it coherence and meaning. "We define the concept of 'situation' by saying that it represents a standpoint that limits the possibility of vision. Hence an essential part of the concept of situation is the concept of 'horizon'. Horizon is the range of vision that includes everything that can be seen from a particular vantage point. Applying this to the thinking mind, we speak of narrowness of the horizon, of the possible expansion of horizon, of the opening up of new horizons, etc.." (HG Gadamer)

It is with this background that we can better appreciate the power of horizon in the experience of architectural space. We are only too familiar with the surprising effect of a change in the floor levels of a room, or in entering a room or building by steps which take us up or down. The role of horizon is even more explicit in view of a broader context, particularly in relation to a garden or landscape, where a part of the space is very often levelled, serving thus as a reference and measure for the rest of the space. The most important aspect of horizon is its ability to preserve the constancy of human situations. The constancy itself has its source in the wholeness of the latent world, the silently structured continuum, in which we live and act spontaneously, and which we share. We experience the wholeness of the latent world as an "alertness that pervades and casts an horizon *vis-à-vis* all present things. It is like light that illumines all lighted things as far as one can see. It is like darkness that cannot be grasped or seen through, dark into dark. It is like a tone reaching the limits of audibility and seeming not even to stop there. It is like a silence that is heard with sounds." (CE Scott)

The surprising degree of integrity and stability of typical situations, preserved under changing conditions and in different places is manifested in the horizon, seen not as an imaginary line but as a structure, which holds together the individual elements of a particular situation by the continuity of reference to the horizon of the latent world. The reference to the latent world, the attempt to articulate its hidden content and richness, the dialogue of "silence that is heard with sounds", are the main intentions of the projects and realisations. Expressed in more specific architectural terms, reference coincides with the much debated notions such as representation, physiognomy, figuration and character. The commitment to the dialogue with the latent world leads inevitably to some form of visible reference to the latent world.

In the work one can see conscious and courageous attempts to address this difficult question. In most of their projects there is a visible tendency to establish a primary order which would meet not only the requirements of the brief, but would also reflect the longer tradition of the ordering of space in our culture. The primary order is not identical with structure, the overall tectonics of buildings or with classicising tendencies, as it may sometimes appear. The structures, to take one example, are always subordinated to the physiognomy of the wall, the texture and material of the surface and the nature of the space. The resulting order can be best described as situational. It is constituted on the level of the visible purpose of individual spaces and their hierarchy. In the extension to Pembroke College in Cambridge, the wall of the students' accommodation wing is not a frame as it may appear at first, but a sequence of spatial layers, establishing an important difference between the external layer referring to the character of the Foundress Court and the deeper layer expressing the private nature of the individual rooms. A similar interpretation can be seen in the office building of Finsbury Square in London, where the external, stone, load-bearing wall addresses the public nature of the city square, while the internal life of the building is expressed through the neutral detached screen of glass behind. The dialogue with the latent world and its visible representation culminates in the effort to achieve a particular character in the design of individual buildings. This effort coincides with the main intention and the ethos of EPA's work.

The unique role of character has to do with the fact that it is the prime, if not the only link, still preserved with a more authentic tradition of representation. It is a notion which has emerged from a humanistic culture, encompassing not only architecture but also painting, literature, poetry and philosophy. Character became part of architectural thinking in the eighteenth century as an equivalent of earlier convenance and *bienséance* (suitability), and even earlier decorum or *prepon* (propriety), which were still closely linked with ethical considerations. The ethical dimension of character is expressed already in the fact that the Greek term for character is ethos. The presence of ethos brings architecture into the realm of humanistic culture, of which it was until recently an indivisible part. The close relationship of architecture and humanistic culture can be seen not only in the emphasis on the ethos of representation, but also in the emphasis on the communication with other areas of culture, particularly those of knowledge and skills. A good illustration is the treatment of the atrium in the office building in Stockley Park, where the skillful detailing and thoughtful choice of material is subordinated to the overall character of the atrium dominated by the mural with the allegory of Europe.

The commitment to design in which the most important contributions of current technology are accepted, but at the same time transformed into culturally relevant and ethically oriented results, gives the practice a unique place on the contemporary architectural scene.

The situations in which hallucinations can take place are limited to certain spaces and media and cannot be identified with the reality of the whole. There are structures in our culture which resist hallucinations. Merleau-Ponty is more specific when he writes "What protects us against delirium or hallucinations are not our critical powers but the structure of our space." The structure of space has its source in the depth of culture and coincides with overall coherence of our cultural world. Because our existence is always spatial, the nature of lived phenomenal space determines the topography, orientation, meaning and the sanity of our existence.

Modernity and the Question of Representation
Dalibor Vesely

An eye for the whole
Wilfried Wang

Awareness of the dense contemporary and historical context, in which architectural practice appears possible, is probably nowhere better provided in England than between the sylvan academic context of the University of Cambridge and the nervously decedent metropolis of London. Eric Parry, whose London practice Eric Parry Architects (EPA) has grown between these poles, has benefited from these extreme exposures. Thus, from the broad critical philosophical discourse centred around the Department of Architecture at the University of Cambridge have emerged positions in distinction to the exuberant reception of technology as a stylistic and symbolic base for modern architecture, in distinction also to the libertine repackaging of motifs from present and past, favouring instead an architecture of situational poiesis that attempts to immerse itself without prejudice into a given condition.

Dalibor Vesely and Peter Carl, co-teachers with Eric Parry at Cambridge, have over time compacted their critique of a historical and contemporary perspective of architectural theory and developed a philosophy of a situational interpretation, partly based on these of phenomenology (Merleau-Ponty) and partly on the humanist notion of the duty towards the conceptual and formal coherence of artificial expressions, which itself has been transformed in religious, cosmological, political and aesthetic terms. In this sense, the practice of architecture by EPA, is framed by the intellectual critique of theory and praxis and grounded in the cumulative exposure to the profession and society. Thus engaged, EPA does not only

have an outwardly observant eye for the whole, ranging from the urban to the detail, but more pertinently, an inner eye for the undercurrents in contemporary culture and theory.

Furthermore, there is an awareness not only of contemporary architecture but of that which has already been built, at home and further afield, providing an incomparable basis for critique and analyses. EPA is a practice that has gathered individuals from many cultural backgrounds and with diverse experience, a phenomenon not uncommon to the world's multi-cultural cities at the turn of the twenty-first century. However, there is more to this than the dominant, ineluctable cultural context—Eric Parry's biography itself naturally assumed that this would be so. Thus working in the Far East or continental Europe is no cultural problem for a small practice such as EPA, contrary to the majority of other firms in England.

Collaborators from different backgrounds and knowledge of architecture from different regions and different periods distinguishes this practice from most contemporary offices. This broad base has provided a more relaxed approach to that which architectural critics, theoreticians and journalists have called "history". An architectural phenomenon, regardless of its year of completion, reveals its quality not through some ennoblement by means of a label, but by immediately sensed inherent qualities. Such qualities can be describes for those observers unsure of the origin of

their delight, a critic might even provide an interpretation of why such factors help to define quality, but they must be objectively there. The architecture projects, when closely studied, demonstrate these objective qualities; aspects of which have been discussed here in subsequent texts on the key works of the office.

The collection of buildings and projects published in this monograph represents the work of one and a half decades. Its pre-history evidently extends further back in time, though that is not the subject of this monograph. References to significant influences are included where necessary, encompassing the formative aspects of the practice. More generally, the cultural context of England during the last quarter of the twentieth century was shaded by the economic and political decline of a once powerful industrial and diplomatic nation; the financial markets in the political enclave called the "city" and tourism to this anachronistic, imported royal household remained. Other continental states had progressed almost unnoticed by the island's media, and the blinkered version of the "land of hope and glory" was uncomfortable only to those who had experience of life beyond the White Cliffs. The England of the last quarter of the twentieth century was a society in early transformation from industrialisation to commercialisation, that is, to the domination of everyday life by accountants, "who know the cost of everything but the value of none".

A careful socio-psychological analysis of the backgrounds of the first clients would underline their unorthodox nature. Whereas the mainstream 'British' clients wishing their private residencies to be designed by an architect would always, even today, prefer to renovate almost unnoticeably an existing Georgian house in the well-to-do boroughs of London, few would dare to buy a site and have an existing house completely remodelled or indeed have it demolished and replaced by something entirely new. A similar preference is visible with established corporate clients. While those large developers operating in the financial centre, the City of London, still defined by a mixture of Medieval privilege, guild dominated patronage, a decadent political system, a moribund church wardenship, and a working population of a quarter of a million set against a resident population of some six thousand, have understood the need to provide modern offices, the pressure of tourism and middle-England have given an incisive voice to unreconstructed classical reconstructivists, headed by a member of the royal household. The endless controversy surrounding the environs of St Paul's Cathedral is the principal example of the schism—in more than a stylistic sense—in the self-understanding of the cultural state.

England's architecture during this last quarter of the twentieth century had few buildings to show that encapsulate and express the dilemma of changing mores and lifestyles. The rawness of *béton brut* architecture, propagated for instance by the London County Council in their social housing by Ernö Goldfinger in north Kensington or Alison and Peter Smithson's Robin Hood Gardens in east London, that had been a fixation during the 1960s, had been misappropriated by cost-minimalists in public bureaucracy and was quickly "sent to Coventry" and demonised. Insensitive infrastructural projects such as the Westway A40-M40 raised motorway in north Kensington caused lasting planning blight to an already insanitary area of central London. The South Bank Arts Centre with its 1960s additions of the Queen Elizabeth Hall and the Purcell Room (by the architects of the Greater London Council) completed the symbolic death of Brutalism. Le Corbusier's name, being associated with this aesthetic preference, was beginning to lose credibility amongst the English public.

Alison and Peter Smithson's Economist Building in St James, 1963, one of the most complex and refined urban schemes ever to be built certainly in England if not anywhere in the world, was taken for granted by an underinformed public. Urban design in England had, until the end of the twentieth century, not seen anything remotely equivalent in terms of design quality. Without it, however, such sensitive compositions as Arup Associates dormitories at St John's College, Oxford, and subsequently Pembroke College Students' Rooms and Master's Lodge and Damai Suria would have been all the more difficult to achieve.

The dearth of non-housing related public buildings during the subsequent years (one notable exception being Denys Lasdun's National Theatre complex at London's South Bank) provided at least for students of architecture the freedom to phantasise. Parallelling the continuing museum and cultural centre programme in Germany, schools of architecture set seemingly interminable designs for such cultural facilities, a phenomenon that may well have been of benefit to the end of the millennium, lottery sponsored inflation of cultural institutions in England.

Media attention to the early work of Wendy Foster, Su Rogers, Norman Foster and Richard Rogers of the 1970s gave the impression that out of the constant misery of industrial decline, a new Zion, called "high-tech", might emerge. Young architects close at hand witnessed, however, how craft dependent this high-tech architecture was. The grand figures such as Leslie Martin, Patrick Hodgkinson, Bob Maxwell, Reyner Banham, Kenneth

Frampton, Joseph Rykwert, Alison and Peter Smithson, Philip Dowson were increasingly incommunicado, some emigrated to the USA. James Stirling celebrated his practice's return to media attention with the controversial Schinkelesque extension to the State Gallery in Stuttgart, a building of a scale and significance that could only be realised outside England and the foundation for a project for a practice whose designs would largely be carried our in the basement of a central London Georgian house but built beyond the shores of England. With the death of Stirling and the ennoblement of some of the high-tech architects, usually a distinction that marks the zenith of the recipient's career, the last decade of the twentieth century became an open field for the advancement of the next generation.

However, to many observers, whether students of architecture or mere interested lay persons, the conditions for the successful trajectory of an architectural practice remains a mystery. Which strategy should a practice pursue in the awareness of the glamourous spectrum of built work? What chance does a small, young practice have against the star system? In what manner should contemporary thoughts and theories be integrated into one's own work? What of the practical side of the profession: management, the construction industry, craftsmanship, materials, liability and insurance, social skills? How are those barren years full of eagerness on behalf of the architects and pitiful commissions on behalf of penny-wise clients bridged? How does one secure an important project? How does an architectural practice ensure continuity with ever significant assignments? Ultimately, how does a practice define and achieve architectural quality?

In the case of EPA, there were unusual as well as conventional circumstances that affected the practice's development. Founded in 1985 on the basis of small and intensive interventions such as renovations of apartments and offices, the office followed the traditional, gradual steps of engaging in the small-scale, entering large-scale competitions and slowly building a reputation for itself. One of the unusual circumstances in the trajectory of the practice was its inclusion in an exhibition held at the obscure 9H Gallery in Central London in 1987, when, on the opening night, Eric Parry met Stuart Lipton, chairman of Stanhope Properties (one of the most prominent developers in England of the late twentieth century), who later commissioned Eric Parry to undertake a series of smaller and larger designs (such as the office building for Stockley Park, the unbuilt Amenity Building at Chiswick and a private house in London). In the exhibition catalogue, which included the work of three other by now prominent London practices, the architectural critic Colin Amery aptly summarised the work of EPA as expressing romantic and poetic desires in their projects,

referring specifically to a mythic past that is encapsulated in translated references from distant and modern precedents such as Pompeii and classical modernism. Amery far-sightedly and somewhat cautiously suggested the following in his essay: "Parry has an intellectual approach to design that demands a parallel understanding from the client—his academicism is likely to bring about fundamental changes in modern architecture if he can match his arguments with craftsmanship and care in execution." The four exhibited practices were seen by Amery as being inspired by the Modern Movement but having "moved away from the reductionist phase of that style".

The explicit and built criticism of international modernist architecture prevalent in the late decades of the twentieth century, both from an urban as well as from a object-based perspective, gave rise to a variety of abstractions that successfully integrated references to the immediate past as well as to ancient roots of architecture. As previous turns of the centuries had witnessed two well publicised forms of stripped classicism—that of the French Revolutionaries, Louis Boullée and Nicolas Ledoux and that of Central Europeans such as Adolf Loos, Auguste Perret and Peter Behrens—so there were renewed attempts in the aftermath of the anti-modernist debate to rekindle the practice of classical orders and typologies in the 1980s and 90s.

Without entering into a discourse as to the cyclical nature of these restorative phenomena, the underlying intellectual and theoretical frameworks of these restorations suggest a more insistent and continuous, if less immediately visible engagement with the more significant process of formal abstraction. In this context, abstraction can be understood as a multivalent process in attempting to encompass traditional meanings and formal references as well as renewing the eidetic quality of the thus abstracted form. Knowledge and experience of these icons of stripped classicism have made their presence felt in EPA's designs. Beyond these obvious names of classical modernism, to scholars of the process of abstraction in architecture, the buildings and projects by Nicolas Hawksmoor and John Soane were as weighty an influence as those by the continental Europeans. Hawksmoor's Clarendon Building in Oxford, 1713, for instance suggests implied pillars by means of the simplest of recessed, foreshadowing, so to speak, the *architecture des ombres* of Boullée's Funerary Monument, c 1784, and Soane, whose use of recesses extends even to the definition of ornament, as for instance the 'meanders' and 'flutes' in the implied pillars of the arcaded loggia to his own house in Lincoln's Inn Fields in London, of 1813.

Particularly Soane's spatial layering, a peculiarity that would be left unconsidered in relation to the orthodox discourse on layered space by modernist architectural historiographers, predates much that has been claimed subsequently as having been an original thought in this sense (that is to say, the discourse on literal and phenomenal transparency). Soane's studio in Lincoln's Inn Fields, complete with its separation of columns from the perimeter walls, its attached stairs and economic use of space (the legroom beneath the apprentices' drawing boards), the continuity and discontinuity of space by means of clerestories, mirrors and openings (breakfast room), many of these compositional devices can be seen in the project of Eric Parry's setting of Friedrich Dürrenmatt's play *The Physicists*. Here, Parry used the ambiguity of implied openings to symbolise the apparent freedom of the self-confessed but pretending lunatic physicists, who are actually held in a prison. Soane's bewildering spatial conception, perhaps a miniature version of Piranesi's *Carceri*, can be thought to have been a suitable alternative inspiration for Parry's stage design. Undoubtedly, from the House of the Physicists to the Chapel at the Château de Paulin there are kindred architectural thoughts and thus transposed inspirations.

In an earlier project, in which Eric Parry had collaborated with Doug Clelland on a small headquarters building for a computer company (Solid State, Oxfordshire, 1981), such multivalent embracings of architectural history and the specific examples of classical abstractions are discernable. These were furthered subsequently when Parry worked with Dalibor Vesely on a number of speculative projects. The exceptional aspect of Eric Parry's intellectual background and his broad and profound interest in architecture ensured a long teaching engagement at the Department of Architecture at the University of Cambridge from 1982 to 1997. There the discussions with his colleagues such as Vesely, Peter Carl, Peter Blundell-Jones, Andrew Saint, Nicholas Bullock and many others had a lasting influence on his differentiated and critical view of the reception of modern architecture. The cross-influence between teaching and practice should not be underestimated in the intellectual speculative development of an architectural practice. While of course early projects, whether undertaken for competitions of for one's own benefit, are as formative in the definition of a practice's profile, the continuing search that is possible within the liberal domain of academia allows one to find theoretical answers to questions normative practice may not have yet asked or may not be in the position to put.

Towards the end of Eric Parry's long teaching assignment at the University of Cambridge, the results of one of the last diploma unit's design work were exhibited and published in a book entitled *On certain possibilities for the irrational embellishment of a town*. Parry's theme for the diploma unit, the design of what in French terminology are called *équipement*, a word that exceeds the technological dimension inherent in the English meaning and points towards the humanist act of donating an element of public infrastructure, enabling it to take possession of the public domain, a humanist act beyond welfare state paternalism. Students designed small-scale, not to say minuscule objects such as a vendor's box, a writing booth, pavement lights, drinking fountain, daybeds or the leaner.

Labelling the idea of embellishment as "irrational" in the context and with the full awareness of modernist technocracy is a self-ironic characterisation. How else should one introduce concerns that are to be shared in public in an age of neo-liberal technocracy, in which the public realm and the public itself is held in general contempt by dominant media and even so-called progressive political forces? For Parry, the diploma studio was a crystallisation of his long held belief in seeing architecture as a confluence of personal design sensibilities with the identification of collective responsibilities. An architectural edifice, a piece of *équipement*, to Eric Parry is more than a symbolic gesture: an urban artefact engages fundamentally in the daily life of the public, implying that architectural design can be responsible and communicative. The students of the diploma unit were by necessity forced to investigate the appropriateness and durability of the chosen materials, their manufacture as a one-off as well as their other dimension as mass produced items.

In the academic context of Cambridge, the prevalent intellectual critique of contemporary civilisation, specifically the shared interest in phenomenological hermeneutics, was acknowledged in Peter Carl's introductory essay to the publication to have been inspired by Dalibor Vesely. The student work "colonised the gap between the customary theoretical extremes of public and private". Phenomenological hermeneutics "is a 'bottom-up' arguments which immerses itself in the messiness of praxis, its conflicts and accommodations. It is an insight which runs counter to the proclivity for totalising theoretical generalisations embodied in extravagant imagery and language by which modernism—from Le Corbusier to the recent advocacy of 'flowspace' as a vehicle for freedom—has regularly offered salvation from a life deemed ignoble, disorganised, unhealthy, slow, out-of-date, lacking in coherence of purpose."

Aside from Eric Parry's own evaluative comments of the students' approaches, the subject of the studio speaks of his sustained interests, analytical speculations and fascinations. The intensity with which a relatively small design object, such as an urban artefact, can be studied is not initially

Master of Light and Materiality
Adolphe Appia.

top left and right:
Tristan et Yseult, 1923,
Décor du Deuxième Acte.

bottom left: Parsifal, 1922,
Un Décor (Zaubergarten).

bottom right: Dessin de
Rythmique—Die Treppe, 1909.

15

obvious to most non-designers. However, the truth is, that the smaller an object for public use, the deeper its design needs to be rooted within that society's culture in order to become commonplace. Buildings, by comparison, are paradoxically easier to design, they can more likely be subject to the private whims of the architect. The interface between a small object and a member of the public is immediate and more intense, that between a building and a member of the public offers more tolerance. Parallelling the diploma studio in the summer of 1996, EPA was involved in the Southwark Initiative, for which it proposed the refurnishing of a sensitive urban interchange, culminating in the detailing of street furniture such as benches and pavement patterns. While most self-respecting, ambitious architects would turn up their noses at such commissions for economic as much as for publicity reasons (most magazines ignore small-scale designs), EPA have given such an "irrational embellishment of a town" continued and intense care. The unarticulated fascination that can be sensed by those involved in the design is in turn palpable on visual or physical contact with the artefacts at Southwark.

At the Department of Architecture the teachers' idols had for many decades been Le Corbusier and the great Scandinavians, Alvar Aalto and Sigurd Lewerentz. Leslie Martin and Colin St John Wilson, the long serving professors during the last half of the twentieth century, shared this devotion, a fact visible in their principal designs (Bodleian Law Library at Oxford University and the British Library, respectively). The aesthetic of the neo-Brutalist, a term coined by the Swedish architect Hans Asplund— Erik Gunnar Asplund's son—in 1950 in reaction to a concise house design by Bengt Edman and Lennart Holm, much later popularised by Reyner Banham in his book *The New Brutalism*, 1966, was a widely shared Franciscan sensibility (in distinction to the reductiveness of the machine aesthetic), that had inspired Martin and St John Wilson and Alex Hardy at the Department of Architecture at the University of Cambridge, 1959, an extension to the terraced houses containing the school of architecture, has led a life in a time warp, only to be rediscovered by the generation of architects at the turn of the twenty-first century.

The aesthetic sensibilities of EPA developed from here. For example, some of the earliest interventions at the Château de Paulin (the tool shed, the master bedroom and the staircase in the renovated tower), show their affinities to the concrete formwork of Le Corbusier (Maison Jaoul or the Unité d'habitation, Marseille). In the late 1980s, such references were either unknown, forgotten or most distinctly out of favour. Few of EPA's contemporaries sought to root their implicit objection to a material

postmodernism in the resuscitation of brutalist principles of picturesque (in the proper sense) ontological construction: Tim Ronalds, Florian Beigel, and much later Adam Caruso and Peter St John are some of the noted protagonists thereof. Much of the architecture of the late 1980s and 90s was smothered in terms of diction by bland elegance, ideally suited to the expansive boutiqueisation of interiors even beyond the confines of the retailing world. EPA had thus established one important founding element in its architectural discipline in the material construction of architecture (as ridiculous and as redundant as it may appear, but the pervasive use of render, plasterboard and paint as the lowest common constructional elements has reduced construction to an invention of speechless shapes).

In the materialisation of architecture then lies one fundamental root to its ontology. All that follows thereof is subject to the Kahnian question as to what the material wants to be. Yet, given the modern tradition of layered construction, such a position is increasingly difficult to sustain in large projects requiring rapid assembly and off-site prefabrication. The office building by EPA on Finsbury Square is an example of how the principles of construction have been nurtured from the earliest experience with massive masonry at the Château de Paulin to that some two decades later. At Finsbury Square, the masonry is treated in a manner in which stone would want to be today. The remaining fabric, however, follows orthodox assembly methods. That EPA is not toeing the Ruskinain line of constructional didacticism has been made clear since the Southwark Needle, which depends for its structural ability on internal and invisible steel tie rods, a technology that has ancient roots, here contained within a modified form. With continued exposure to unusual craftsmanship thanks to the complexities and refinements of the commissions, EPA have been able to penetrate the search for form beyond the external sensory effect to ask from within the cultural question as to how the material needs to be. In this sense, EPA's approach to architecture could be said to differ from the buildings of the minimalists, notably the work of the 1990s in the Swiss-German region. There the constant reference to orthodox modernism even at the height of postmodernism has cultivated a zealous adherence to the forms of purism, the enshrinement of Le Corbusier as an architect who, while proposing problematic urban schemes, could do no wrong in architectural terms.

Evidently, Le Corbusier remains a strong influence in the work of EPA. Their competition entry for the Welsh Assembly unmistakably harks back to the grand gesture of Chandigarh. The play of seeming opposites: the

18

orthogonal or angular box with the 'free' sculptural form is a theme implicitly acknowledged across the work of Le Corbusier's admirers. Even the furniture, the benches for the Welsh Assembly design follow this dialogical principle of sculptural form against orthogonal frame. Small Corbusian details can be traced here and there in the realised work of EPA: the pool reclining seat in the Mandarin Hotel Spa relates to the resting seat in the Villa Savoye, the window openings and benches in the semi-public space in Damai Suria suggest the sculptural possibilities of a Corbusian nature, the *béton brut* reference has already been mentioned.

Similar to the interest in so-called secondary figures in the case of classical architecture, where Nicholas Hawksmoor and John Soane tend to have a regional significance, even though the body of their work deserves far greater attention than that of the orthodox architects of their time—that is, for instance, Bernini or Borromini and Schinkel, respectively—EPA have studied the work of Eileen Gray, Berthold Lubetkin and Serge Chermayeff, the latter's two buildings, the Finsbury Health Centre, 1939, and the House near Halland, Sussex, 1938, have informed the offices at Stockley Park, while Gray's ingenious furniture pieces have inspired EPA not least for the work at the Lipton Residence, London. The three latter architects could be argued to represent the poetic and humane face of modern architecture. Specifically the critique expressed in the work and writing of Eileen Gray, brought back to international attention in 1971 by Joseph Rykwert, in *Perspecta* 13/14, resonated with many minds critical of the unquestioned reception of orthodox modernism. Undoubtedly the research into the work of these so-called secondary figures strengthened the intellectual acuity of interested architects, also providing them with a panorama that had hitherto seemed to be restricted to a few names. Precise investigations into the motives and attained results further encouraged ambitious students to investigate these alternative trajectories. Particularly Gray's work, and not only her furniture designs, demonstrated that invention is possible, necessary and exciting, provided that the grounds for its unfolding are properly prepared. The designs, especially in the case of well-budgeted domestic projects, but also in the case of the Spa, reveal this dimension of design.

Coincident with the critic of technocratic modernism is EPA's interest in the picturesque properly understood. Thus, the office on Finsbury Square is unthinkable without the numerical mysticism of the proportional system for the lower fenestration developed by Yannis Xenakis in the case of Le Corbusier's Monastery at La Tourette, 1960, John Week's further development of these ideas in the design for Northwick Park Hospital, 1964, (see

particularly the reduction in the number of mullions on the upper levels) and Rafael Moneo's Town Hall for Murcia, 1998. EPA have fused the concerns of structural efficacy and honesty with those of an apparently more irregular, relaxed composition in their design for the openings of the Finsbury Square office. In contrast to the more Gothic principle of stepping piers, transposed to the twentieth century in the work of Ludwig Mies van der Rohe (Promontory Apartment Block, Chicago, 1949) and later on by the Smithsons (Economist Building), the changing cross-section through the self-load-bearing facade pillar, while holding to the building line, is a classical design principle (as for instance seen in the layered orders of the Colosseum in Rome). Architectural order as a conceptual-structural concern is understood by EPA in terms of an abstracted tradition of the classical orders. Here the historic field of influence of Italian and French Renaissance treatises (Alberti, Sebastanio Serlio to Blondel) on English architecture (Jones, Vanbrugh to Soane) is still noticeable. Pembroke College Student Rooms and the Finsbury Square offices can be placed within his domain of thought.

At a spatial level, the concerns have been for the differentiated enclosure of rooms. This differentiation ensures that a room is not axially determined, that there is no prerequisite direction other than the dominant dimension of a space. Comparing three designs, this approach becomes evident: in the House for the Physicists, the core space is surrounded by stairs, pillars and landings—symmetries of one side of a room are not echoed on the other, thereby creating a rotational unfolding; the treatment rooms of the Mandarin Spa, calm in themselves, are bounded by a variety of subtly articulated surfaces (including the ceiling) clad in different materials, complete with openings (doors and windows) in non-concurrent positions; the principal rooms of the chapel at the Château de Paulin are bounded by a similar variety of articulated planes, all with asymmetrically located windows or doors. Thus, such spaces are smoothly defined, they are calm but not static.

During the first two decades of EPA's practice, certain compositional preferences have become apparent: logically emerging from the discipline of abstracted tectonics, configurations express a repetitive, though on occasions carefully varied order—alternative designs for Queen's Grove, Pembroke College, the Welsh Assembly, Damai Suria or Finsbury Square—in which the weight of the primary constructional material determines the poise of the building, a poise that sometimes faces counterpoints as agents of articulation (as for instance the recessed glazing plane at attic level of Finsbury Square).

Homage to Friedrich Dürrenmatt, Villa of the Physicists, project 1986.

The two buildings in the most complex urban setting are Pembroke College and Damai Suria. Both reveal the mastery of balancing the pressures from the inside and out, from the site and the public at large, neither denying the scale of the overall developments, nor permitting the complexes to become overbearing, monotonous or rigid. The earlier reference to the relevance of the Economist Building for the articulated configuration of Pembroke College and Damai Suria is to be understood from this point of view: the Economist high-rise is almost invisible from the streets of St James; its sitting to the rear of the plot ensures the respectful continuation of St James; the changes in the grid dimensions on the facades of the three different configurations plays with the perspectival effect between similar objects, helping to diminish the impact of the tower still further. Pembroke College Student Rooms mediate between the grand clearing of the College's green and the smaller grain of residential units to the south. Similarly for Damai Suria: the lateral wings are located in those positions that, on the one hand, maximise open space and, on the other, tie the complex into the existing fabric.

From the choice of material, to the development of the detail, the establishment of a tectonic order, the control of spaces and the articulated distribution of a building's mass, EPA are in the process of developing a complex, refined and differentiated architectural language. Without the almost obsessive and intense care given to the earliest commissions, EPA would have slipped into the bland and orthodox trajectory of a typical architectural office. As the practice has proven, thanks to the diligent development from *L'architecture en miniature* to *les grand projets* (Granta Park, Finsbury Square, subsequent office buildings), it is able to cover the traditional spectrum of architectural design, including the "irrational" design of urban furniture, for any building type. While such a statement may appear self-evident to some, given the dominant condition of contemporary professional practice, in which specialisation is common and systematically encouraged, if not to say enforced, this ability of EPA is becoming increasingly uncommon. EPA's direction, its experience in academia and practice, have shown that balance between realms of freedom and discipline as well as wide exposure to technologies, craft skills and materials establish one footing of a successful practice. However, for it to contribute to the development of architecture, conscious and self-critical positioning within the vast range of possibilities is only possible through the engagement with reflective discourse. In this sense, EPA is an unusual practice.

While it may be wiser to await the realisation of the next generation of buildings by EPA before drawing any broader conclusions, the built and designed evidence to date suggest that EPA is an office concerned with the conscious embodiment of culture. The work demonstrates an awareness of decisive strains of history—here understood as a continuous phenomenon, not one that terminates with a phenomenon's inclusion in a publication—and thus with a particular evaluation of these strains. From these evaluations emerge an understanding of contemporary civilisation with its attendant culture—here understood as a broad set of anthropological rituals and values, and not as an exclusive, canonic—emblematic set of symbolic events. Architecture's tendency to be absorbed in the mechanistic thoughtlessness associated with terms such as value engineering, mass production, just-in-time delivery and other technocratic jargon better suited to the construction of cars than primary objects of culture, which buildings are, or at least ought to be, has been recognised by EPA, and the disembodying dangers that such spiritless mechanisms pose for the practice of architecture have been met by EPA in the manner herein outlined. Taking note of the acclamation that continues to meet, on the one hand, so-called high-tech architecture with its claims to realising 'intelligent', 'ecological' buildings, and, on the other, photogenic pseudo-minimalistic designs, EPA's position is difficult to hold. EPA have proven that they can "match the arguments with craftsmanship and care in execution" (Colin Amery's gauntlet to EPA). EPA's goal of realising an architecture that poetically embodies the culture of contemporary civilisation despite the continued division of labour, responsibilities and construction systems is a high one.

e
pa

volume 1

Contents

Artists' Studios
London

Hidden behind large steel gates, the two studios for the artists Antony Gormley and Tom Phillips gather around a yard, establishing a coherent urban quality unlike much of the surrounding area.

ground floor

Antony Gormley
1. dark room
2. clean area
3. lead working studio
4. sculpture studio

Tom Phillips
5. etching studio
6. entrance/exhibition space
7. yard

first floor

Antony Gormley
1. office
2. painting studio

Tom Phillips
3. painting studio
4. library

Mezzanine floor
5. portrait painting studio

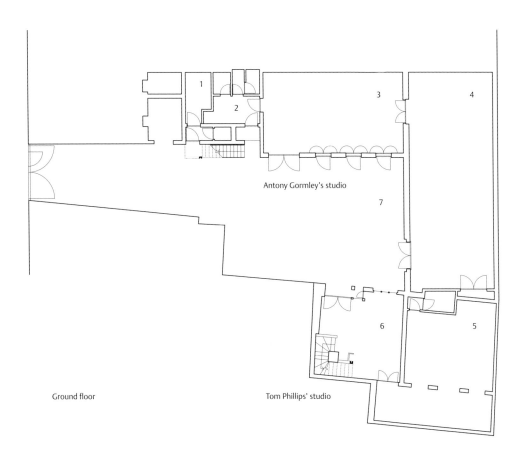

Antony Gormley's studio

Ground floor   Tom Phillips' studio

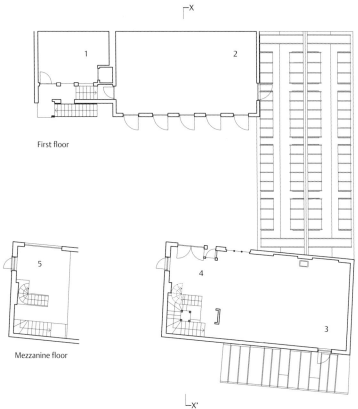

First floor

Mezzanine floor

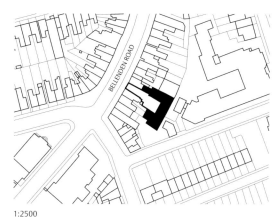

1:2500

Bellenden Road, Peckham, is a quirky and somewhat run-down version of the English High Street, a commercial street lined with shops, such as newsagents, grocers, butchers, hairdressers and second hand car dealers. The mixture of late Victorian and neo-Georgian terraced houses, the amalgam of narrow, hopelessly overloaded streets winding their way from the inner city to the never ending suburbs that have long ago invaded the home counties, the general tawdriness of much of this urban fabric that in total considers itself one of the world metropolises, all help to define the impression of a neglected order constituted from the private realm.

In such a world of irregular plots and ground floor grocers shops, the veil towards this private ordering system is rarely lifted. Thus the inner sanctums of block interiors, brutally revealed when viewed from the railway viaducts severing this type of London fabric, is only known to locals, map readers or estate agents.

The courtyard site, a typical left over space at the tip of a triangular block, accommodated at first a laundry, then a garage. Its presence is only noticeable through the gap in the row of shops. Subsequent additions of sheds and lean-to structures obscured the central space, they were removed to make way for the new yard. The studios for Antony Gormley, the sculptor, and Tom Phillips, the painter and graphic artist, occupy two of the existing double-storeyed buildings on the site. Gormley's studio was complemented by a single space workshop with zenithal lights set in a double-pitched roof. Faced with a heavily rusticated brick wall, two tall oak doors set into the wall at the southern end give access to the courtyard, while a further pair on the interior connect the workshop to the tools area such that a balanced internal elevation is established. Thus a monumental wall terminates the approach from the street and connects the two more articulated entry buildings to either side.

Different to the simplifying designs of the Modernists of the 1930s or the strict order of the Italian neo-Rationalists of the 1970s, Parry expanded the exploration of deep facades as means by which the lack of depth of openings—a loss due to economic rationalism of the early twentieth century—could be revived in a coincidental way with the accommodation of circulation and loading functions. In the case of the Gormley studio, the access stairs are placed on the outside, creating an ambiguous volume, on the one hand, in line with the side wall of the terraced house on the street and, on the other, aligning with the existing two-storey studio. The upper flight becomes partially enclosed, giving a protected entry to the studio proper.

turn the dark lamp

Tom Phillips' illustration of Canto XXVIII of Dante's "Inferno". Bertran de Born holds his severed head like a lantern bearer. Phillips transfigures the landscape of the ninth gulf into an image of destruction based upon his own memories of the London Blitz. Otherwise titled by Phillips *A House Divided* the idea of vertically fractured fabric was the basis of the tower.

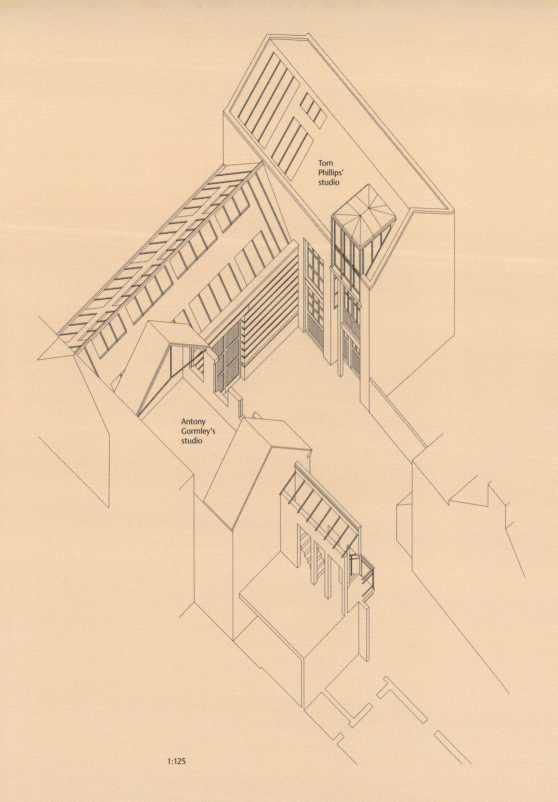

Tom
Phillips'
studio

Antony
Gormley's
studio

1:125

left: Axonometric.

right: The courtyard, Tom Phillips'
studio to the right; Antony Gormley's
to the left and doors to the large
studio centre.

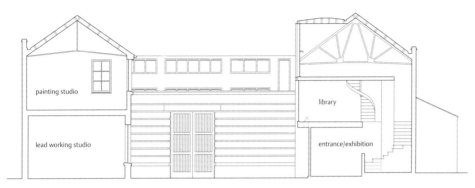

painting studio

library

lead working studio

entrance/exhibition

section X–X'.
1:200

On the opposite side, the tower of doors and windows for the Phillips' studio has a recessed ground floor volume providing a loading bay to the upper floor through a slot in the first floor. The rectilinear dormer topping this vertical element marks the end of the courtyard's enclosure. This tower of doors and windows is complemented on the interior by a stairwell that winds around a miniature museum. In fact, such is the condensation of accommodation that all volumes, whether enclosed or lined, provide drawers, niches, bays or balconies for objects (Phillips' collection of African votive sculptures) or people. With such concentration of space use, Parry has detailed the enclosing and lining fabric with minimal dimensions. Moreover, the fineness of window mullions or balustrades, the slenderness of the asymmetrically placed post at the entrance, the proportioning of all the small gaps in relation to the metal or wooden sections create a density that stands in opposition to the expanse of the thus liberated main compartments.

This is an approach seen in the work of Adolf Loos and Eileen Gray. It is the principle that a tight space, which overlooks a more generous space, is able to be significantly smaller than the norm would suggest. The image of *St Jerome in his Study* by Antonello da Messina, well known to all educated in the range of the School of Architecture at Cambridge University, is an earlier exploration of this phenomenon of extreme introversion in relation to spatial opulence. The theme of *l'architecture en miniature* of the built furniture *qua architecture* in St Jerome's study is already present in an abstract form. Few mouldings or details suggest a temporal connection to the Gothic interior, a further act of removal that isolates St Jerome in his own world.

Seen from this vantage point, the relation between Parry's interventions, each circulation and service component adjacent to the actual spaces of production and assembly are concentrated explorations of depth and movement. As such they participate with the interior as much as they mediate between inside and outside. It is fair to claim, beyond the benefit of hindsight, that these early explorations in the essential qualities of form and space have left their mark on subsequent projects.

Arguably then, the stairwell and landing of Tom Phillips' tower of doors and windows becomes a visionary condensation of a theme to come. Originating, in part, in the topos of the recluse—ancient and classical ivory tower, imaginative domain of the artist—Parry's choice of an abstract language for the forms that make his *l'architecture en miniature* can be seen as both liberating from the then current debate of the postmodern and as connecting to the mode of abstraction as seen in the Messina painting of St Jerome. The tower is of its own a series of frames set within a frame. The recursions of these frames extend from the display cases to the courtyard, revealing how Parry has the whole in mind.

left: The painting studio was considered primarily as a top-lit introspective room with a controlled view into the courtyard at the tower end and a window at the other end (deliberately too high to look out of).

right: Initial sketch.

left: Tom Phillips' studio with the more compressed spaces of the tower beyond. Again, a grid in the floor provides a way of measuring the room and understanding its scale.

right: Initial sketch.

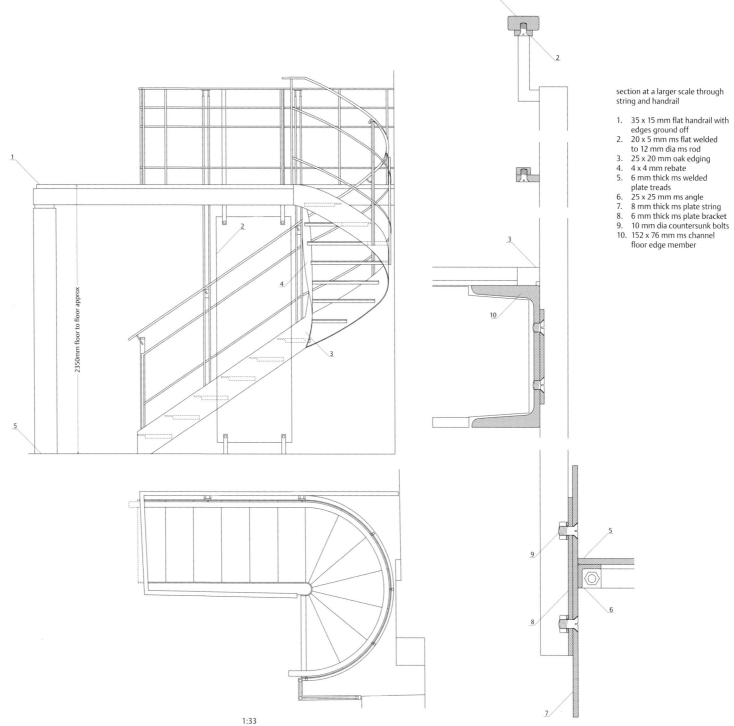

elevation and plan of staircase at mezzanine level

1. new mezzanine level
2. 6 mm toughened glass balustrade
3. welded seam, ground smooth
4. 102 mm dia x 8 mm thickness chs cut on site to form string for spiral section of staircase
5. existing floor level

section at a larger scale through string and handrail

1. 35 x 15 mm flat handrail with edges ground off
2. 20 x 5 mm ms flat welded to 12 mm dia ms rod
3. 25 x 20 mm oak edging
4. 4 x 4 mm rebate
5. 6 mm thick ms welded plate treads
6. 25 x 25 mm ms angle
7. 8 mm thick ms plate string
8. 6 mm thick ms plate bracket
9. 10 mm dia countersunk bolts
10. 152 x 76 mm ms channel floor edge member

2350mm floor to floor approx

1:33

top: Tom Phillips' studio. Stair to mezzanine.

bottom: Tom Phillips' studio. Stair to main studio from ground floor.

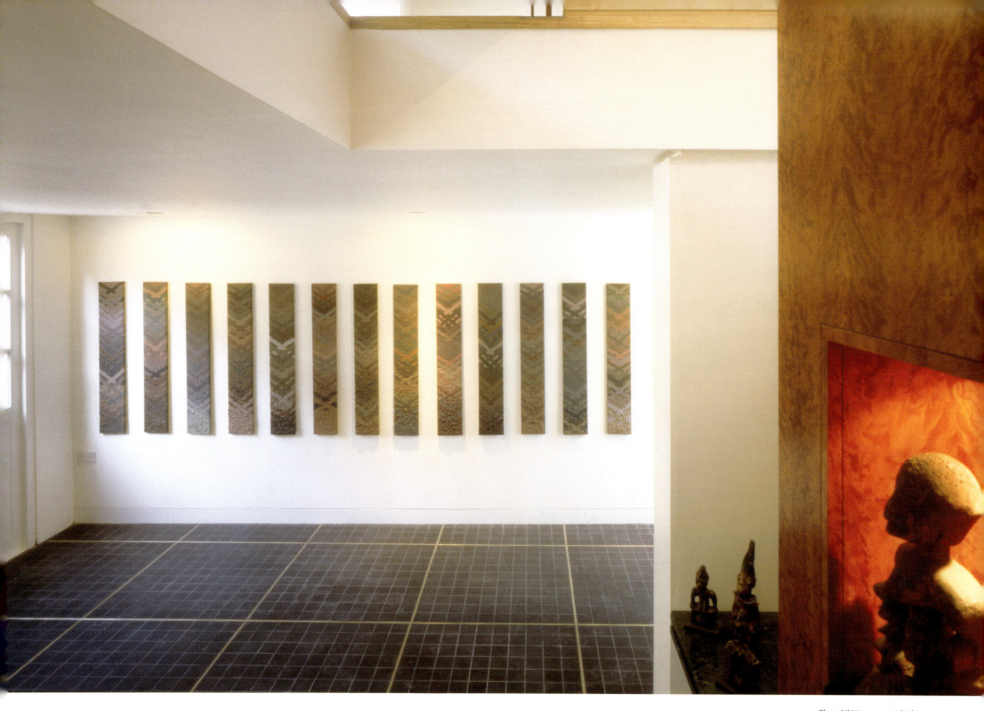

The exhibition space at the base
of the stair now has its first layer
of accretions. The brass inlay in the
floor reveals the irregularity of the
old building and the consistency
of the new work.

Views of Antony Gormley's sculpture studio.

Château de Paulin
Tarn, France

The rehabilitation and extension of a château in the south of France, northeast of Toulouse, perched on top of volcanic outcrops that form a deep valley with cliffs and more tempered embankments, has been a continuing project over the course of almost two decades. Interventions range from basic conservation of the fabric, new buildings, fittings, furnishings, to a private museum for prints and manuscripts.

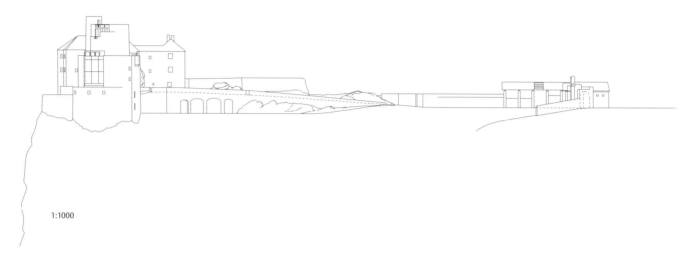

right: West elevation. To the left is the edge of the outcrop 200 m above the valley base. Section X–X'.

1:1000

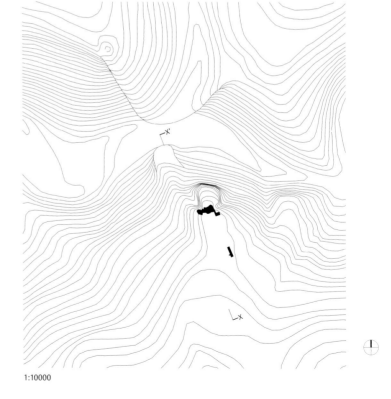

previous pages: Photo collage of the existing building in 1986. The building is the accumulation of parts added to the defensive rock outcrop from the eleventh century onwards.

above: Two early twentieth century photographs of the château. Of note is the building with the conical roof which has since collapsed. The rock outcrop is a treeless landscape, very different to the heavily wooded condition of today.

right: Location plan.

1:10000

The origins of the Château de Paulin date back to the eleventh century. Its modest size and its almost non-existent defensive layers suggest that it was no more than an idealised hermitage, clothed in a monolithic world of small openings and intermittent terraces.

Today, the château is a manorial retreat with a generous and grand, but nevertheless domestically scaled series of rooms and halls. Its historical development is decipherable from the fragments included in the masonry: an early Medieval dungeon and much of the wall construction at ground level around the tower, a late Medieval barbican, the late Renaissance upper floor above this together with parts of the eastern wing, with more muted, contemporary rehabilitations and extensions of the curvilinear tower complete with the chapel-cum-museum.

Since the mid-1980s Eric Parry Architects have undertaken the design work for the château from the London office in collaboration with a large number of local contacts. Early submissions to the responsible *architecte du patrimoine*, the authority in charge of overseeing development to conservation sensitive buildings, have established the necessary credibility in the design work of the practice and given them the required elbow-room for all of the subsequent alterations. Craftsmen from the area have been in charge of the masonry and concrete works, as well as occasional carpentry, while most of the fitted furniture and steelwork has come from London.

The outstanding quality of the masonry is due to the expertise of the cathedral masons, whose profound knowledge of the local stones and the comprehensive understanding of detailing and design have been an invaluable resource for the project and the architects' own continuing education. Undoubtedly, it is through this project that EPA has been able to develop details and designs for contemporaneous and subsequent schemes, such as Pembroke College, the needle at Southwark or the self-load-bearing facade for the Finsbury Square office building.

The unique geological condition of an overhanging stone outcrop, rising almost vertically, has been the cause of much human self-overestimation. Components of the château have been constructed close to geological fissures, that have given way partly under the weight of buildings, partly as a result of progressive weakening due to weathering. Thus, collapsed fragments of previous buildings were retrieved from the foot of the outcrop following the change in ownership in the early 80s and have since been used in the construction of various wall sections around the château.

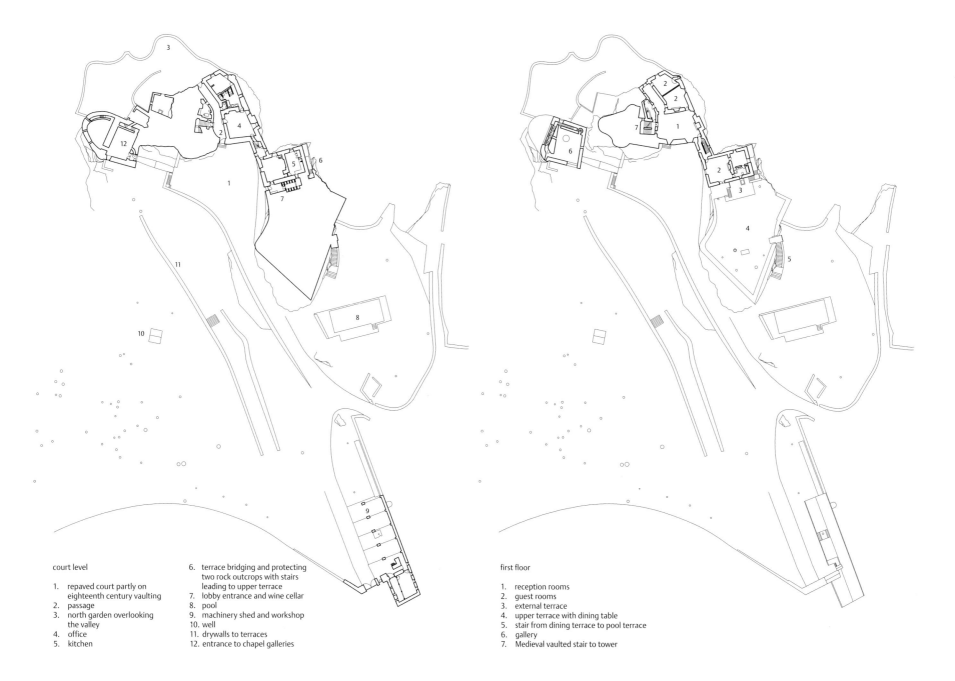

court level

1. repaved court partly on eighteenth century vaulting
2. passage
3. north garden overlooking the valley
4. office
5. kitchen

6. terrace bridging and protecting two rock outcrops with stairs leading to upper terrace
7. lobby entrance and wine cellar
8. pool
9. machinery shed and workshop
10. well
11. drywalls to terraces
12. entrance to chapel galleries

first floor

1. reception rooms
2. guest rooms
3. external terrace
4. upper terrace with dining table
5. stair from dining terrace to pool terrace
6. gallery
7. Medieval vaulted stair to tower

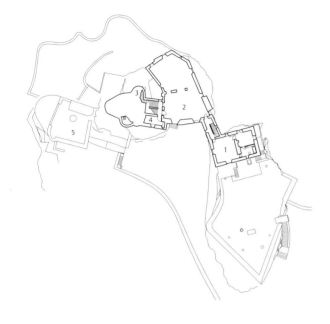

second floor

1. study and bedroom
2. gallery reception room
3. new stair to tower
4. barbican
5. terrace

1:1000

View of the east elevation of the château after restoration of its walls and during construction of the tower.

The design involvement has been comprehensive, if not immediately evident. A new entry next to the new tool shed complete with dovecot welcomes the visitor. New terraces with dry stone retaining walls and a new front court on top of specially constructed dry stone arches establish a continuity between the gate and château, at the same time, the stonewall terraces interweave the artificial domain with the topography. To the left of the short driveway, set on a cleared embankment is a new stone enveloped swimming pool, whose western edge acts like a weir, giving the swimmers the impression of being able to swim close to the edge. A new curvilinear wall containing a storage area underneath connects the lower pool area with a clearing that can be used as an external dining area, surrounding this are fountains and sculptures by Steven Cox, whose work has also been incorporated in the Mandarin Oriental Hotel Spa.

On the northern side of the château, a number of new balconies and terraces extend the perimeter presence of the building and complete the circulation route around and through the complex. On its interior, a new kitchen has been installed, a wine cellar incorporated beneath the kitchen terrace, and significantly, the timber floor has been reinforced and sound insulated. This involved the separation of the beams from the battens, inserting steels on top of the slotted beams and creating an interstitial space between the old ceiling boards and the timber flooring. All of the windows have been sensitively reframed, with the vents in the Renaissance balustrades being glazed.

Most visibly, the curvilinear tower to the northwest has been completely overhauled and reconfigured with a recessed balcony looking westwards over the valley. A geometrically controlled sweeping spiral staircase rises to the master bedroom in the tower. Having been able to appreciate this view for some years, the decision was made to capture the same view from the new 'museum', this time with the drama of the topography unfolding at first hand: the promenade is composed in such a way as to lead the owner or visitor past a double-height glazed window whose edge condition expresses the cleavage of the rock below, indicating that the construction beyond this glass plane may literally fall away without notice due to the unpredictable fragility of the geology.

Summarising the interventions, their most noticeable quality is their subtlety and utter recessive character. Much of this is due to the patina that the stone has assumed over the decades, giving the château the sense of a uniform age, even though some of the details speak of different origins. Distinction is sought on the western facades of the new top of the tower and the new museum, here the contemporary nature of the composition is most obvious. EPA have thus achieved an impression of calm stability towards the approach sides, where everything is made as if it were a uniform coat that suddenly shows a gap on one side only, thereby revealing its 'true' physical condition. Thus EPA have been able to grant the château and its setting a new lease of life.

Table in Indian river granite slab.

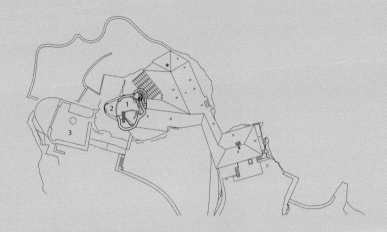

tower level

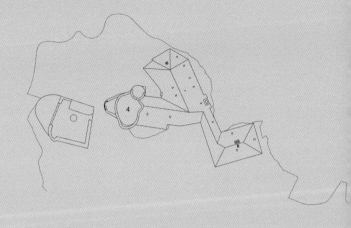

roof level

1.   tower room
2, 3, 4.   roof terraces

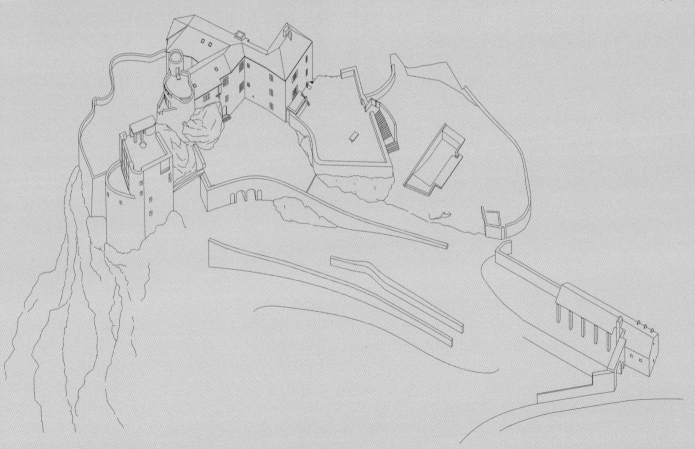

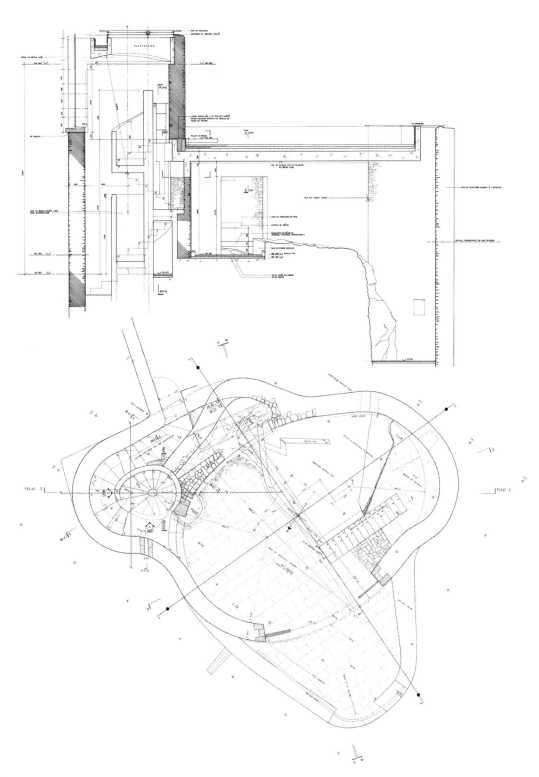

Working drawings
of the tower project.

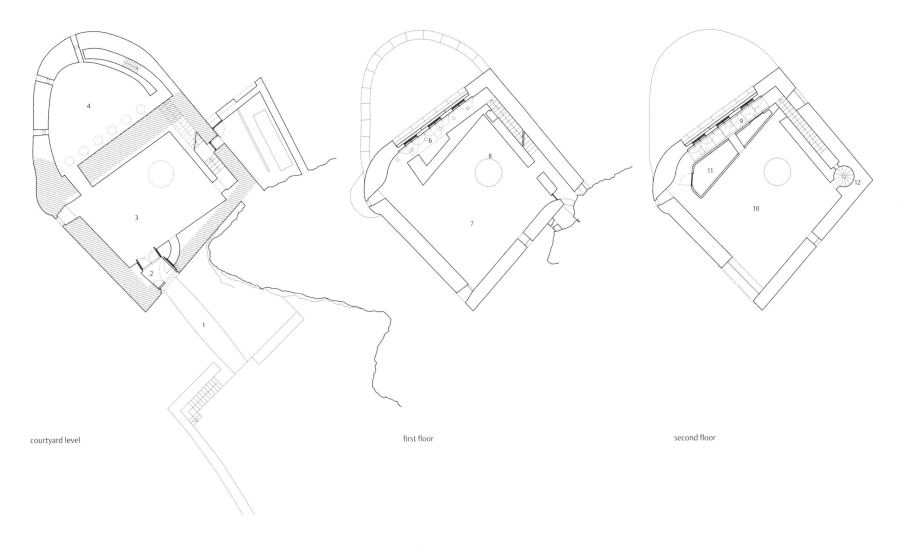

courtyard level

first floor

second floor

1. bridge to entrance
2. wind lobby
3. gallery
4. room
5. passage to existing cell
6. passage behind environmental wall x existing
   stonewall 2 line of probable collapse
7. gallery
8. oculus and trickle ventilation slot
9. glass bridge
10. gallery
11. store
12. stair to roof terrace

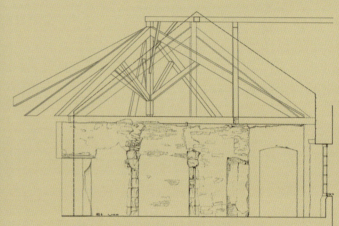
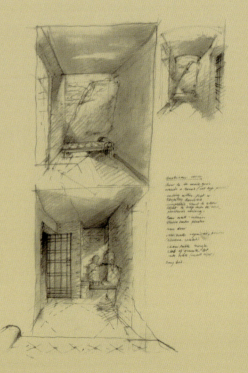

opposite left: View of the spiral
stair leading to the tower roof
terrace, under construction.

opposite top right: Survey
drawing of the roof and fire
damaged walls.

opposite bottom right: Sketches of
proposals for the barbican room.

Planning application elevations
as proposed.
top: West elevation.
bottom: East elevation.

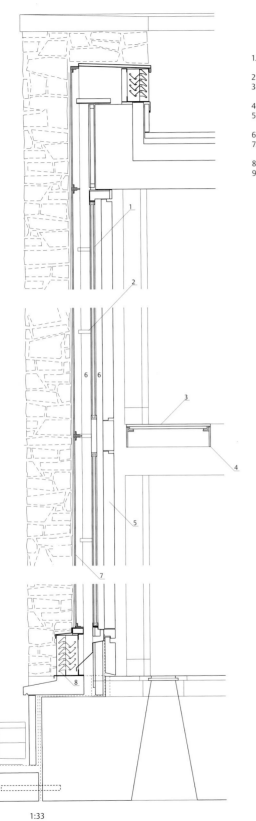

1. 6-12-6 DG unit in Sapphire glass in metal frame
2. SS 300 rods to carry 3
3. two layers 19 mm Sapphire paired interlayer glass
4. mild steel edge beam
5. reclaimed pitch pine screen wax finish
6. ventilation cavity
7. 12 mm toughened Sapphire rainscreen
8. 150 mm toughened Sapphire
9. colt triple blocked 3UL louvres

1:75

1:25

1:33

1. outer rain screen
2. inner timber screen
3. openable double-glazed units
4. glass bridge
5. lens lights

1. outer rain screen
2. inner timber screen
3. openable double-glazed units
4. primary structural steels

Office Building W3
Stockley Park
London

Just a few miles north of England's largest airport, Heathrow, a major transformation of contaminated land formerly used as a waste dump into a business park was conceived by one of London's most intelligent developers, Stanhope Properties. Stockley Park, as the office development in an extensively landscaped setting is called, is now the base for technology businesses taking advantage of the immediate vicinity of the airport, the M4 motorway and the neighbouring golf course. The developers made a clever decision in so far as the untested reaction to a site next to the airport would suggest excessive noise from airplane activity; that is not the case. The planes tend to land east–west, and the site is due north: their continuous arrival and departure at intervals of one minute makes for a silent choreography of metallic dots on the horizon.

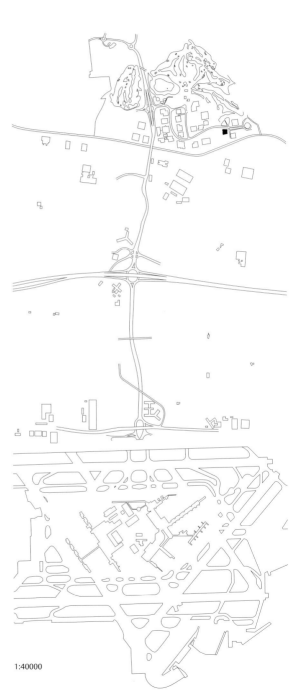

1:40000

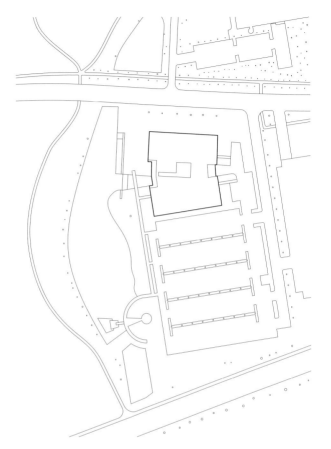

1:2500

left: Location plan showing the M4 running east to west with the link to Heathrow south and Stockley Park and the new golf course north. W3 is indicated top right.

top right: Site plan. The south wing of the building adheres to the masterplan rule that buildings should be aligned 9° from north (see location plan). The north wing was aligned with the road as the building was to act as a threshold to the second phase of the development.

bottom right: This early sketch shows a number of embryonic ideas. At this stage the entrance is indicated from the centre of the north wing. The stretched space between the north and south wing was beginning to find an echo in the form of the storm water lake to the west of the building.

With the overall plan laid down by Arup Associates, numerous outstanding pieces of low-rise speculative offices were erected across the site. Ian Ritchie's trellised glass case, Arup Associates' sail protected steel and glass boxes, Norman Foster's double cantilevered steel framed interpretation of Louis Kahn's Kimball, and subsequent double-glass structures by Arup Associates as essays in low energy consumption, can be seen across the now densely planted setting.

Few developments on such a scale in the proximity of the greater environs of London managed to survive the commercial vicissitudes of boom and bust throughout the 1990s. In the course of transforming from a society with a clear emphasis on traditional industry, Britain, and especially the catchment area around London, saw the closure of steel works, coal mines, ship building yards, dock yards and car manufacturers. The central role of a global financial market was consolidated during the 1990s. Thus with de-industrialisation, on the one hand, and the growth of the financial services sector, on the other, the demand for new office spaces for a variety of recently established companies had grown. The more sophisticated amongst these start-ups were interested to match their financial appeal with a representative space; and it has been technology companies that have sought to match the image of the building in which they work with their self-understanding. Stockley Park and its buildings offered a complex of images: the modern office

building set in a late version of the English landscape garden tradition of winding roads, curvilinear water elements, vegetation to match, all within convenient reach of rapid local and international transport systems. They were the elements of success, with Stockley Park coming out ahead of other ambitious business park developments in terms of timing and attractiveness for tenants.

The two-storey offices were designed on the tight developers brief to provide for various combinations of lettable floor spaces. The Stanhope 'double bar' type accommodates a central entrance area, generally an atrium that serves as a point of orientation and as an access system for the potential variety of tenants. A car park is located on the building's perimeter.

However, this architecture differs significantly from the so-called high-tech imagery of neighbouring office buildings. It was this difference that interested Stuart Lipton, the head of Stanhope Properties. Lipton was keen to see whether an architect, whose work to that date had no corporate offices to show, but was rather regarded by the professional press as being intense and poetic, could bring an attractive alternative to an area of development that has hitherto been considered mechanistic. As fate would have it, Lipton and Eric Parry were to continue their relationship with a series of buildings and projects that would include Lipton's own house in north London.

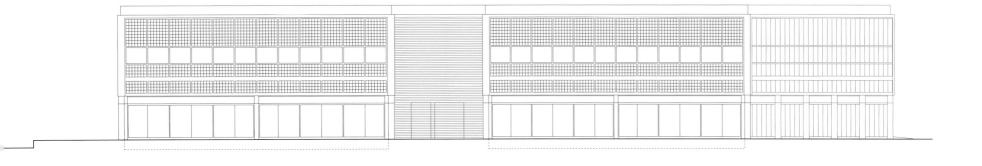

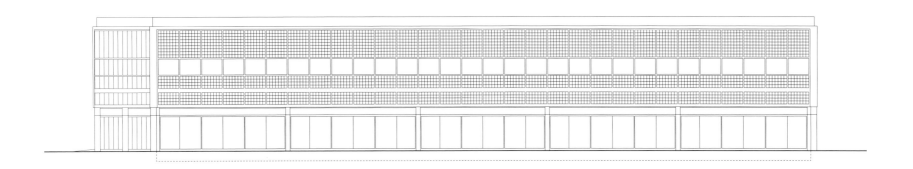

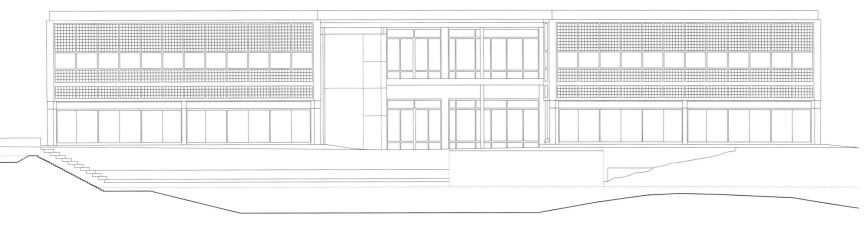

1:250

56

opposite top: East elevation with louvered wall to the plant room between the wings.

opposite centre: North and south elevations (symmetrical). Dotted lines indicate floor levels 800 mm below external ground level to reduce the area of external cladding.

opposite bottom: West elevation. The central recessed bay houses the entrance whilst the balcony overlooking the lake is also an external fire escape route, with the escape stair housed behind the solid precast wall. The area reached by steps at the level of the lower water basin is a retreat from the office, set between the cascades of water and reed planting.

right: The idea of a glass pavilion is emphasised by the dominance of the first floor 'floating' above the ground floor. The sectional device to create this was achieved by the lower glass block panel masking the floor structure and the normal office ceiling being canted upwards at the perimeter of the building. The fake spandrel described by Patrick Hodgkinson as "naughty but nice" echoes precedents like that of Wren's Trinity College Library in Cambridge.

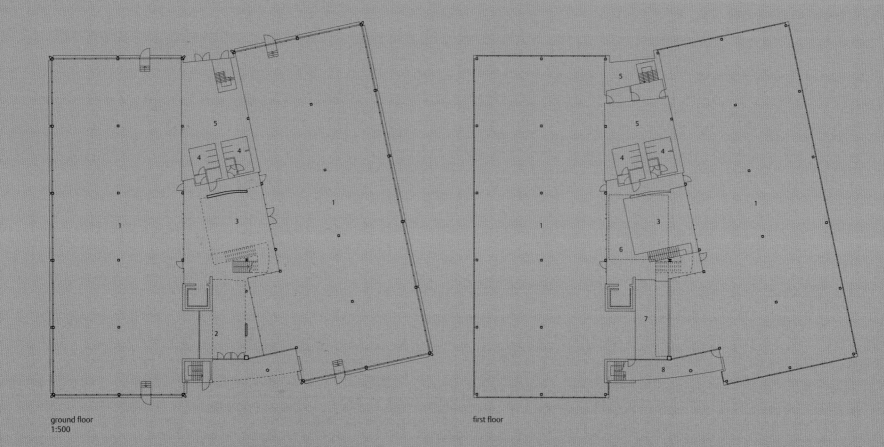

ground floor
1:500

first floor

1. office space capable of
   subdivision into a maximum
   of eight tenancies
2. reception
3. atrium
4. wcs (prefabricated units)
5. plant
6. gallery
7. rooflights (dotted)
8. terrace

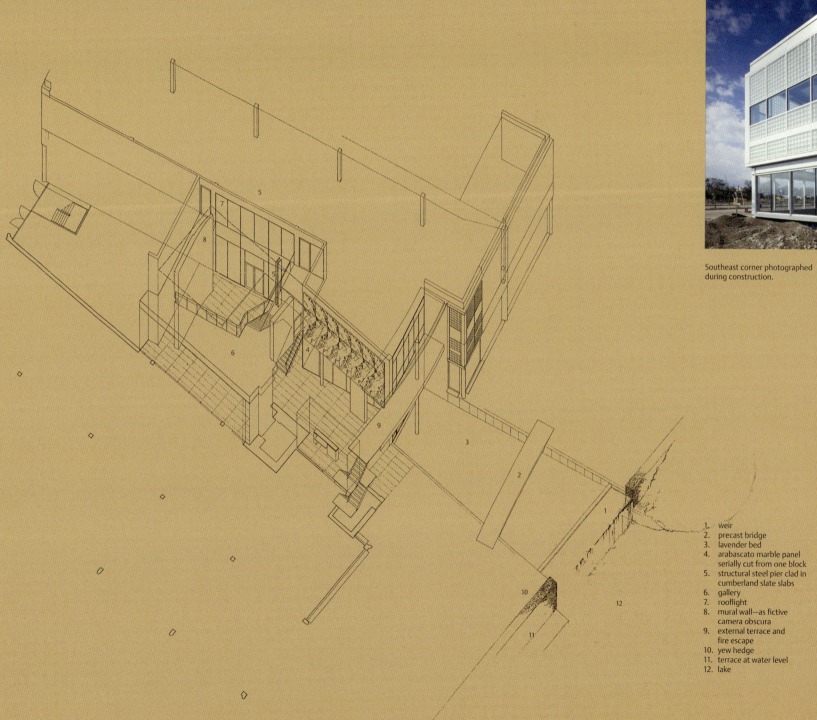

Southeast corner photographed during construction.

1. weir
2. precast bridge
3. lavender bed
4. arabascato marble panel serially cut from one block
5. structural steel pier clad in cumberland slate slabs
6. gallery
7. rooflight
8. mural wall—as fictive camera obscura
9. external terrace and fire escape
10. yew hedge
11. terrace at water level
12. lake

left: A gallery wraps around three sides of the atrium at first floor level. The view across one of the office floors offers a prospect through the clear horizontal strip of glazing.

right: The mural painted on the gentle curve of the exedral wall of the atrium is a kind of mirror capturing a virtual landscape whose theme of foundation, *The Rape of Europa* is depicted as an antidote to the instant landscape beyond. This and other coloured panels were painted out by the first tenants. The entry sequence is now a diluted version of the original.

below: W3 as camera obscura.

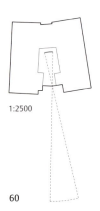

1:2500

For some time, Eric Parry Architects' office building stood on its own towards the western edge of the site, marking the second phase of development; now, the business park has grown and building W3 or No 1 the Square, as it is otherwise known, has become part of the array of gleaming boxes. Taking advantage of the site, the two bars containing the offices proper are set at an acute angle to each other: on the one hand, the southern bar marks the parallel edge to the car park, thereby giving the four rows of hedges structuring the car park a more architectural interpretation, while on the other hand, the northern bar is set parallel to the adjacent road (Furzeground Way). With the concentration of the car parking all in one area, the building as a whole is given a more urban setting, it closes in on the roads rather than being equidistant from road, boundary and landscaping.

The splay between the two office bars then gives prominence to the western facade, which literally embraces the approach road and, more significantly, opens to the generous lake with its cascades and curvilinear edges. Here is thus also a public facade that expresses entry. There is no diminutive entrance porch, but a double-height vestibule leading to an atrium. There is a palpable idea of a link between the office's atrium and the lake, an understandable concept that is achieved by using the metaphor of water as materialised on the exterior by the expanse of lavender being bridged by a low arching extension of the lakeside perimeter pathway and on the interior by the sea of olive green Cumberland slate with its subtle striations laid in the direction of the lake. The building's engagement with the landscape is then the strongest contextual move: EPA's concern with the rooting of buildings in their context, even if this context is entirely man-made and new, in this case instantaneous, allows the building to enter into a scalar dialogue with paradoxical effects. Here is a building that is part of a larger design, appearing at once smaller on its own but bigger when seen as a single composition with the surrounding landscape.

The courtyard in the two artist's studios was a quiet inlet, an urban reserve. Here at Stockley Park, the double-height atrium is an architectural *nature morte*, a vanitas composition of galleries, free-standing walls and murals, stairs, handrails; the composed asymmetries carefully scaled and located to provide a multiple stage for familiar and foreign users. The scale is distinctly ambiguous: fluctuating from the grand domestic to the intimate corporate environment. Here, too, is a purposeful manipulation in scale.

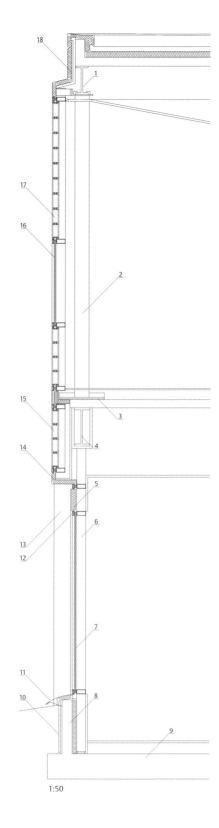

1:50

1. 406 x 178 x 74 mm ub supporting 125 mm roof slab
2. 203 x 203 x 71 mm uc
3. fixing channel
4. 533 x 210 x 82 mm ub supporting 125 mm first floor slab
5. 3 mm pressed aluminium insulated panel
6. proprietary aluminium mullion
7. double-glazed units
8. 150 mm thick concrete, bund wall
9. rc slab
10. 10 mm protective board
11. curved aluminium sill
12. 100 x 60 mm aluminium channel
13. precast concrete pilaster
14. 2 mm aluminium soffit with rock wool (foil backed and taped edges) insulation
15. panel 900 mm high between transoms
16. 24 mm double-glazed units
17. glass block panel
18. silicone seals in aluminium fascias, soffits and copings

top: Cladding under test.
left: typical section through the external wall.

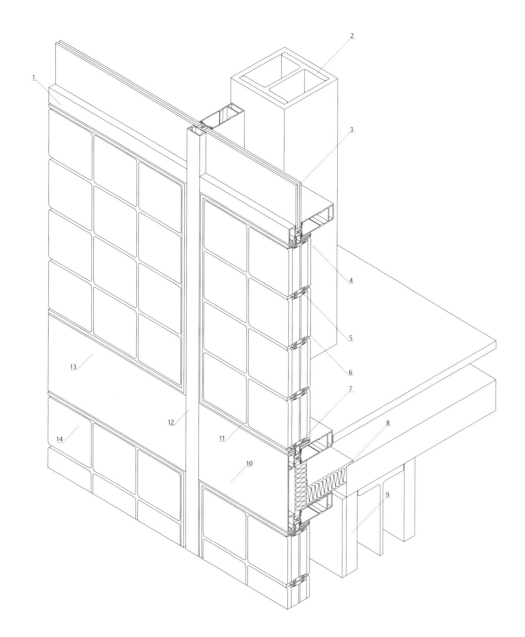

1. proprietary aluminium
   transom
2. columns at 9 m crs
3. 24 mm double-glazed units:
   6 mm clear float glass
   6 mm clear float
   toughened glass
4. panel 900 mm high between
   transom crs
5. clear polypropylene spacer
6. double-bead,
   clear silicone joints
7. 2 No 100 x 138 x 5 mm
   pvc u packers per bay
   drainage holes
8. smoke stop held in wire
   mesh tray with foil top
   returned and adhered
   to insulated tray pane
9. fire protection
10. 245 mm high snap-on
    fascia panel
11. purpose-made
    aluminium section
12. mullions at 1500 mm crs
13. flush aluminium cover plate
14. 197 x 197 x 100 mm hollow
    blocks with fibrous interlayer
    without silicone coating to
    glass faces

1:150

Looking from the upper offices outwards, the surroundings become framed views. The glass blocks, by virtue of their ambiguity with regard to translucency and opacity, in fact accentuate the selectiveness of the view. The receptionist's office at Pierre Chareau and Bernard Bijvoet's Maison de Verre in Paris is clearly one acknowledged reference for EPA so far as the skin is concerned. A source for the external composition could be seen in the white houses of Le Corbusier, principally Villa Savoye. The proportion of the ribbon windows in EPA's W3 building in relation to the ground floor, visibly articulated as a glass screen and rhythmically structured by encased reinforced concrete columns, owes more to the Villa Savoye as the archetype of a two-storey building than to the Maison de Verre. The extension of the glass blocks from the first floor into the clerestorey section of the ground floor offices could be understood to result from such interests in Villa Savoye proportions. Further, the external ground plane is slightly tilted towards the balustrade level of the ground floor, so that it feels well embedded. Conversely, on the first floor, the ceiling is tilted towards the edge beam, so that a more generous spatial feeling is achieved here. Manipulating the sense of enclosure in these different ways, EPA is able to characterise each floor in an archetypal way, bringing to the references their own weighted direction. With the splay in plan, the two office bars are treated as dominant volumes such that the corners are articulated by the three-quarter engaged columns set into a square pillar. In a way, the classical detail of 'engaged' columns is a sleight of hand to achieve a recessed facade at the base and consequently

a projecting first floor in deference to the Corbusian precedent. The Miesian dilemma of how to turn the corner and how to clad it is screened in a dialectical way: structure and cladding play a dilating game of expanding skin and contracting structure, and the engaged columns and pillars are a commentary on the shifting foci. This approach could be argued to also explain the shifting reading of the building in terms of its true interior volumes in relation to the external reading of them. Were the two floors expressed as identically high volumes, the external reading would be more 'honest', but the office would seem less grounded, a critique much used against the dynamism of Le Corbusier's principle of *piloti*—a nautical import in more than one sense.

The use of glass blocks tends to imply a rigorous application of a geometric grid, the ideal of coincidental structural and cladding grids is often implied. The office building W3 has three, perhaps four sets of interlocking grids: the grid of the joints between individual blocks, the grid of the collective panel, the grid of the substructure and the grid of the overall, three-dimensional representative frame. Superimposed on that is the effective reading of window openings, those at ground and first floor. This reading coincides with the grid of the overall, three-dimensional frame, and characterises each double-storey office bar as a large bay-window. In this manner, the privileged relation is based from the interior outwards, giving the occupants a panorama of the site. The building is not about a linear or sectional idea, that would be too mechanical, but

about a presence on site. Embedding the building by establishing a bund to the ground floor, allowing the office bars to project beyond the central core thereby establishing four corners, all these gestures lend weight to the relative independence of each office bar, an independence that is about a precise engagement with the site, and not an arbitrary system that has purposelessly landed on the ground in the middle of nowhere, like some of the neighbouring structures.

Without reading W3 too closely, the observer might conclude that there is nothing all too special about it: yet another office building in a late English landscape garden. One might even conclude that the few detailed and conceptual moves made do not establish sufficient differences between the common office block and W3. Indeed, other solutions to the tight developer's brief might appear visually more exciting. However, none achieve a rootedness as does EPA's design; the building is an essay in commerce in arcadia.

View from the atrium towards
the entrance.

Lipton Residence
London

Without doubt, the fact that Stuart Lipton, one of the most exposed figures in the building industry with a corresponding need for privacy, commissioned Eric Parry to remodel his house in London immediately after the success of the office building at Stockley Park and during the difficult recession years 1991–1994, is more than an act of confidence. This small but intense domestic project and its equally successful completion can be understood as having laid the foundation of the practice's subsequent professional development. Stockley Park and this project (as well as the design for the interiors for Stanhope Properties on Berkeley Square), though limited in scale, are projects that come but once in an architect's career. Their completion to the satisfaction of the client opened doors that are normally only permeable to the established.

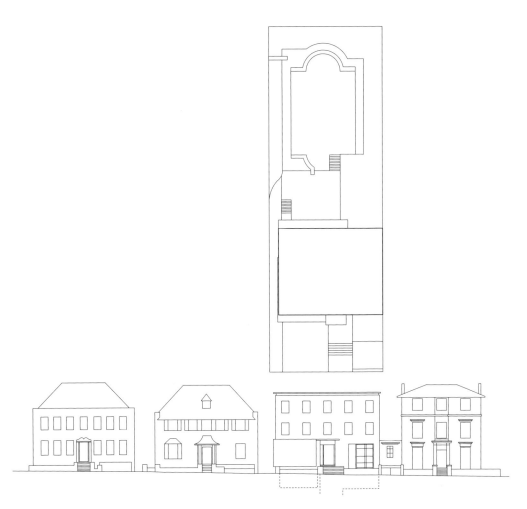

Stuart Lipton's association with a young and relatively untested modern architect are objective aspects of a culture different to the melange of neo-Georgian refurbishments and interior fit-outs that predominate the domestic realm in London.

The original state of the house was that of a typical pretentious neo-Queen Anne house of the 1930s. A three-storey, wide fronted building with a half-sunken garage and corresponding ramp beside the landscaped front garden, the light brickwork, with its subtle mortar joints, sits between the white neo-Georgian terraced houses of Bloomsbury or Knightsbridge and Scandinavian modernist interpretations. With its hipped, double-pitched roof, the house suggests independence, though it in fact is contiguous with its neighbours. The interior prior to the interventions felt small in relation to the outward expression, and this mismatch was the cause of the building's pretence.

From this vantage point, Eric Parry Architects' design has opened the house in three senses, ultimately bringing its outward expression in line with its inner articulation: a clearly perceivable vertical extension via a generous stair from the *piano nobile* upwards and downwards; a screened horizontal extension beginning with the eastern wall of the entrance hall and terminating in the house's new relation with the garden; and the more generous and varied connections between the lower ground floor dining room as well as the kitchen to the terrace and garden at the northern part of the site.

The alterations and furnishings to the first floor with its appropriately scaled, neither excessive nor diminutive, dressing and bathrooms conclude what has been a comprehensive intervention within the fabric of a family's dwelling. The resulting character of the refurbished house could thus be described as having been adapted to the needs of a modern self-assured family that sees the private home as a grand enough meeting ground for the inclusion of the extended family and friends, yet small and manageable enough to just be a home for two.

Unbuilt first proposal for a new house.

68

first floor

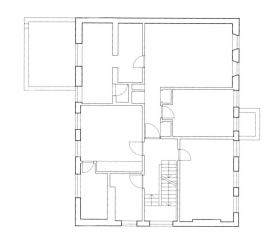

ground floor

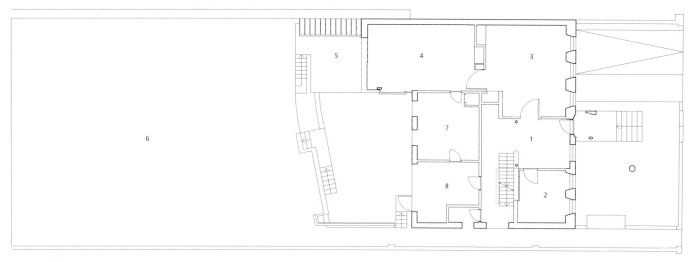

lower ground floor

1. hall
2. study
3. reception
4. garden room
5. terrace
6. garden
7. kitchen
8. day room
9. dining room
10. lower court

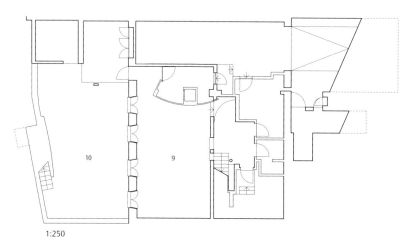

1:250

69

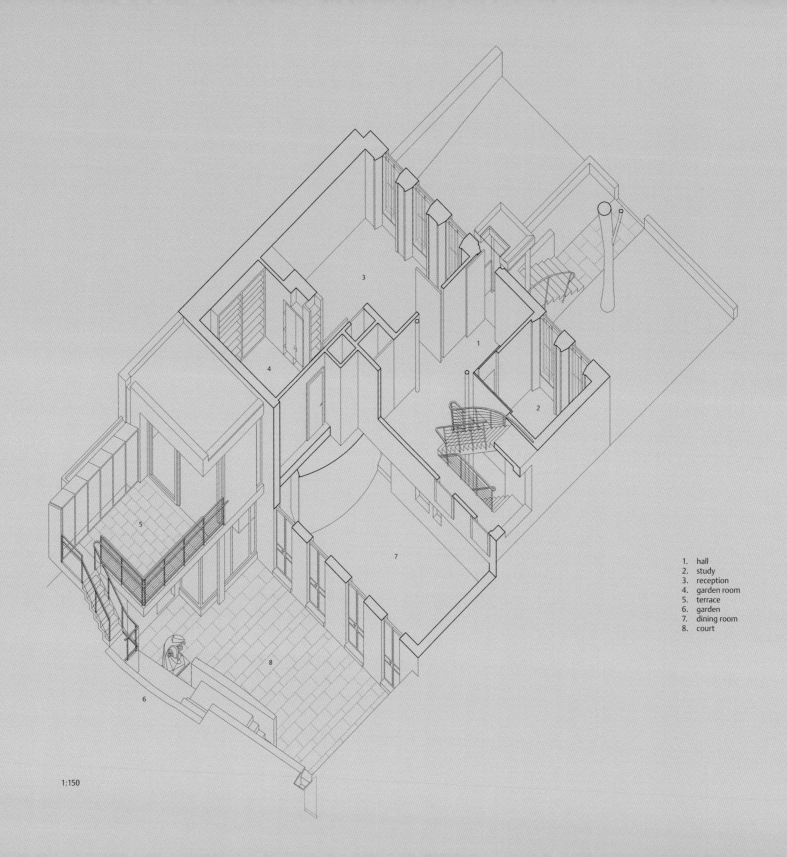

1. hall
2. study
3. reception
4. garden room
5. terrace
6. garden
7. dining room
8. court

1:150

left: Hall view to study.

right: View to bedroom.

left: Garden room, extension and terrace from garden level.

right: Internal view, open corner to terrace and garden.

opposite left:
Court elevation.

opposite right:
Garden elevation.

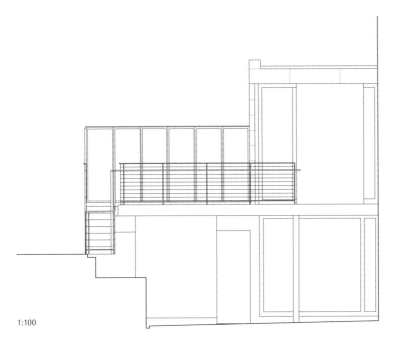

1:100

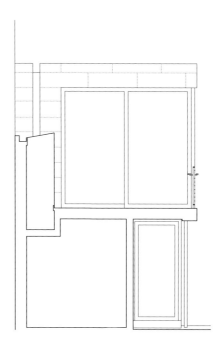

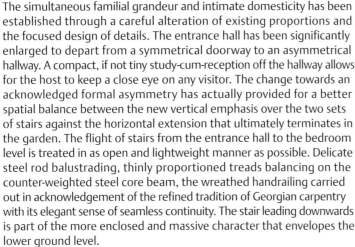

The simultaneous familial grandeur and intimate domesticity has been established through a careful alteration of existing proportions and the focused design of details. The entrance hall has been significantly enlarged to depart from a symmetrical doorway to an asymmetrical hallway. A compact, if not tiny study-cum-reception off the hallway allows for the host to keep a close eye on any visitor. The change towards an acknowledged formal asymmetry has actually provided for a better spatial balance between the new vertical emphasis over the two sets of stairs against the horizontal extension that ultimately terminates in the garden. The flight of stairs from the entrance hall to the bedroom level is treated in as open and lightweight manner as possible. Delicate steel rod balustrading, thinly proportioned treads balancing on the counter-weighted steel core beam, the wreathed handrailing carried out in acknowledgement of the refined tradition of Georgian carpentry with its elegant sense of seamless continuity. The stair leading downwards is part of the more enclosed and massive character that envelopes the lower ground level.

From the entrance hall, a new sequence of living and informal dining spaces stretches to the north, emerging from the rear garden facade with a wall in the form of a botanical case. On the street side, the living room remains introverted with an asymmetrically placed passage leading to the informal dining area, that is integral to the garden room. From here, like a fulcrum, the views penetrate both the house and the garden, without, however, appearing formally authoritarian. The plastic composition of the tectonic elements and the resultant relation to the ground are reminiscent of Eileen Gray's houses in the south of France, the impression offered to the user is that of a unity between the two, eliminating altogether any idea of lower and upper ground floors. The formal dining room thus assumes the role of the house's *sala terrena*, with the external excavated terraced area now becoming a large courtyard. Some of the retaining walls and the terrace itself are clad with Travertine, removing the entire extension from the ascetic neo-Modernism of Tadao Ando, for example.

In other instances EPA approaches the composition and materiality of the house with a sense of recessive elegance. Deep tanned cherry in the dressing rooms lend a nautical association, the precisely detailed fitted furniture of the bathrooms itself recalls the compact luxury of railway compartments or sedan cars. The unfolding shutters and cupboard doors bridge the domains of furniture and architecture. They are traces of the compositional tradition of Gray, which regards every design component as a link between realms of comprehension. EPA has shown with the conversion of this neo-Queen Anne house, that a wide-ranging intervention in a manner that is superficially foreign to the *ductus* of the original can nevertheless not only be complementary, but also something relatively autonomous, a new organism at ease with itself.

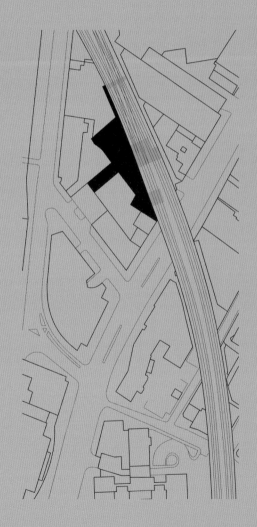

Ministry of Sound
London

The setting for our interventions had already been established for a few years; the long passage, the sound box, the iconic concrete bar. The Club was also established as one of the hot spots of the London Club scene. The location was an inspired use of the 'urban' space between a disused garage forecourt and workshops backing onto and through the brick arches supporting the railway viaduct. From this venue, only open on a Friday and Saturday night, the Ministry has since spread its message globally to an apparently insatiable audience.

The brief was to insert two new bars that reflected the first license for the sale of alcohol that the club had had. As the licensing hours lasted until 2am and the club remained open until dawn, the spaces needed the capacity to transform. The lower bar was designed as a template of the section of the railway arch and the bar within the metal wall was a long slot with a guillotine shutter. Shelves ran along the arch walls to both lean on or perch a drink, and these transformed into a series of banquettes as the room transformed from bar into chill-out space. The upper level bar also acted as a VIP lounge, a dance floor, and party room with its own DJ pulpit. The entry from the gallery overlooking the existing bar, was between sheet metal walls, a third wall tilting into the space was made of crushed metal. Ventilation to the main room was carried through the space in a snaking duct and images could be projected onto floating panels in the darkness of the tall, ceilinged space.

previous pages: MC stage, VIP bar—collage.

Bar/Bed metal frame, stainless steel bar, rubber sheet. In the upright position the furniture acts as a bar ledge and transforms into a banquette.

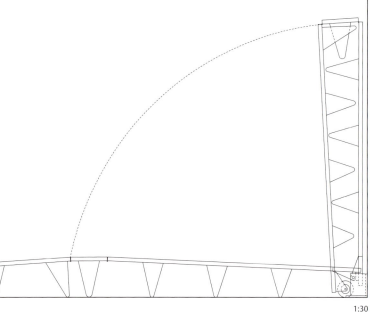

1:30

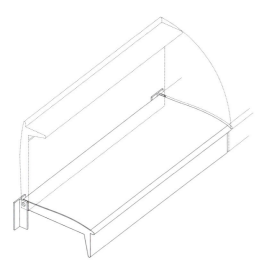

1. bar store
2. the guillotine slot bar
3. bar rest and wall units fold down to form chill-out furniture after 2am
4. actual position of the railway arch
5. slot window in upper arch at raised dance floor
6. vip dance floor
7. bar with retractable hood
8. mc pulpit with crushed metal soundboard
9. triple metal wall entrance
10. projection clouds

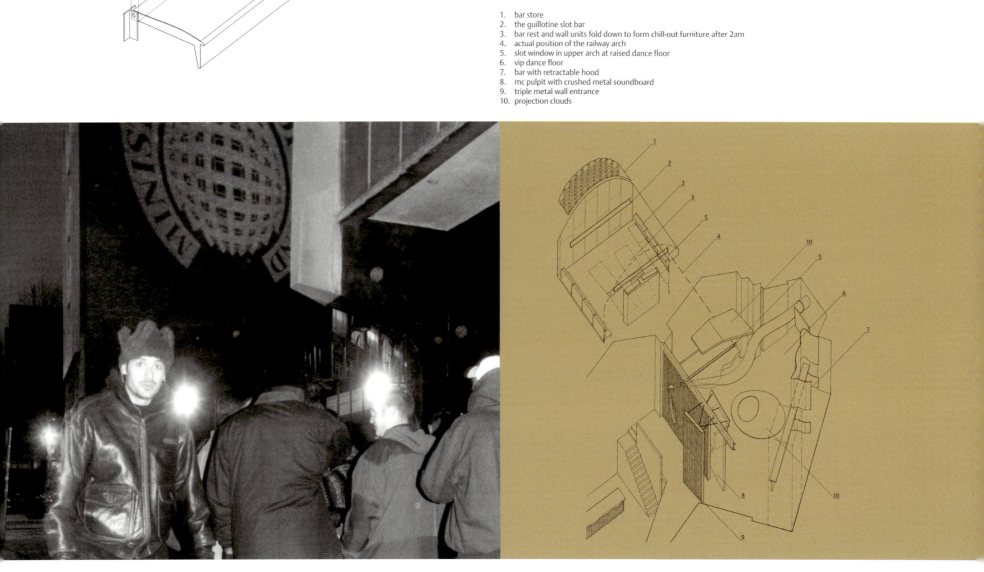

Sussex Innovation Centre
Falmer

The Innovation Centre is a managed workplace that provides a link between academia and commerce in response to a rapidly declining industrial base in Sussex. Interestingly it was a cooperative venture between the two universities in Sussex, two local authorities and local trade and industry ventures. Since opening in 1996 the centre has been nurturing new firms by providing them with the technological and management skills to prosper in the fields of communications, health and ecology.

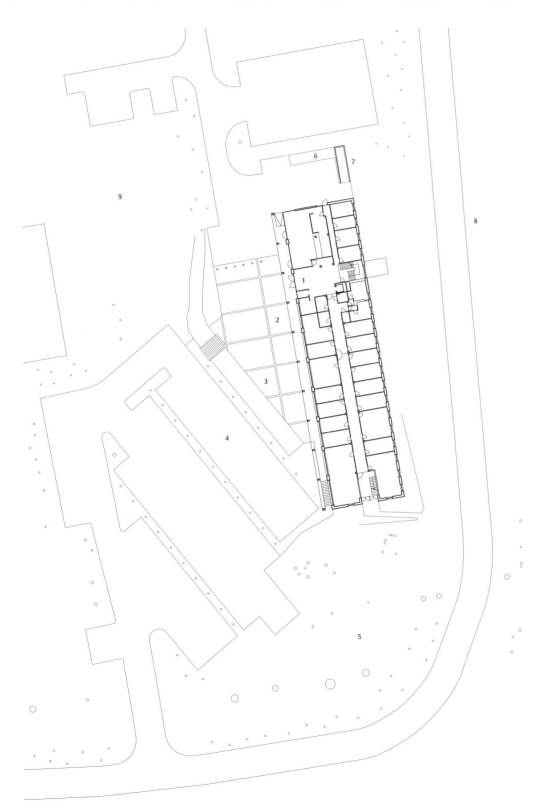

1. main reception
2. concourse
3. retaining wall
4. car park
5. mature woodland with the existing service road beyond
6. bicycle parking
7. recycling bins
8. Tenant Lain, a meadow between the Medieval settlement of Falmer and the University campus
9. site for a phase II building

1:750

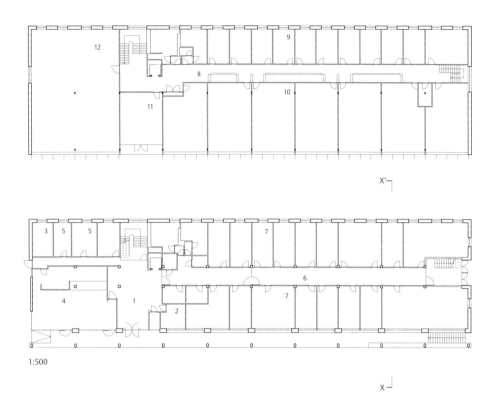

1:500

The building was designed to create an environment that is conducive to interaction on both formal and informal levels, encouraging chance encounters as well as structured meetings. The centre has to be flexible enough to provide for the needs of small offices to larger research laboratories and had to be able to convert from one to the other. The site is on the southeastern edge of the campus of the University of Sussex which was designed by Basil Spence with buildings inserted into a mature parkland. The approach from the main road and railway station created an axis along which the communal buildings in the valley are planned. Pedestrian routes to the faculty buildings ran at right angles up the slope to the east. The Innovation Centre site slopes up to the northeast by 12 m from its lowest point and has fine views across the campus and downs. The idea was to create a building that defined the edge of the campus to the east and a gathering space to the west, a precedent being the stoa of the ancient city. Because of the site section it was possible to place the parking at a lower level to the south bounded by an existing woodland.

The building is 17.5 m wide and 60 m long. The structure of the building is a concrete table with a load-bearing masonry wall at its outer edges to the first floor slab with a steel framework to support and form the roof. The folded plate roof forms a monopitch with a constant eave to the west and a series of gables to the east within which are placed the skylights, ventilation cowls and the single laboratory flue (with multiple ducts). The roof is finished in pre-patinated zinc.

top: West elevation to campus.

bottom: East elevation to
Tenant Lain.

1:250

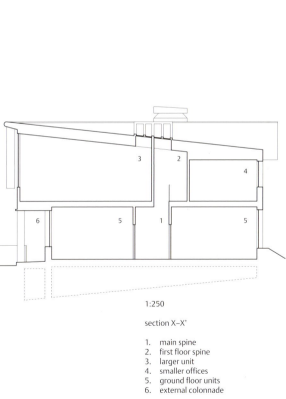

1:250

section X–X'

1. main spine
2. first floor spine
3. larger unit
4. smaller offices
5. ground floor units
6. external colonnade

right: View of the building's
southern gable.

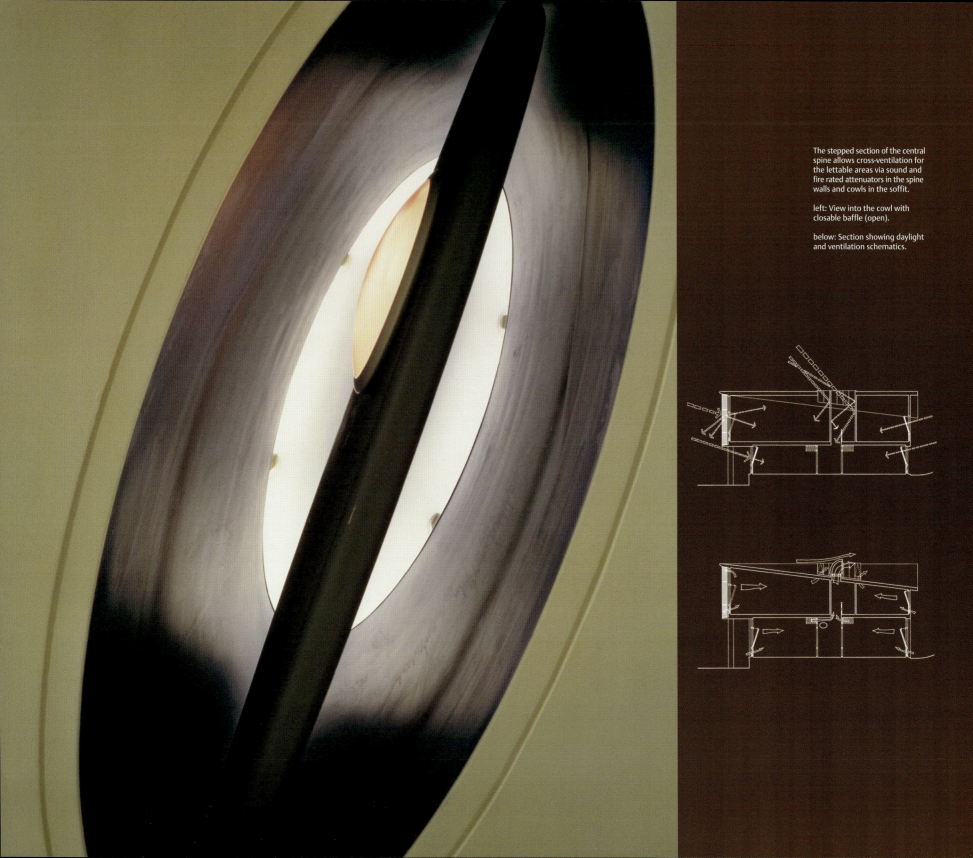

The stepped section of the central spine allows cross-ventilation for the lettable areas via sound and fire rated attenuators in the spine walls and cowls in the soffit.

left: View into the cowl with closable baffle (open).

below: Section showing daylight and ventilation schematics.

left: View along the central spine at first floor level looking towards the main stair. Doors to the lettable units to left and right, with void to ground floor for light and ventilation.

right: View from landing looking up to conference room and down to the entrance.

*New Master's Lodge and
Student Accommodation
Pembroke College
Cambridge*

History is more of a burden for the inhabitants of one of the oldest university towns in England than is generally acknowledged. Nothing expresses this burdensome relation between neighbours, users, planners, conservationists and architects more clearly than the continuing building activity of almost all of the colleges, whether in Oxford, or, as in this case, in Cambridge. Pembroke College, founded in 1347, a few years later than Peterhouse, 1284, and Clare, 1326, was the first to institute the courtyard type, around which all the sustaining facilities would be gathered.

1592

1. Foundress Court
2. chapel
3. library over dining hall
4. Master's Lodge
5. Master's garden
6. orchard
7. Swynecroft—common land

1682

1. Old Court
2. chapel and Chapel Court
3. library
4. Master's Lodge
5. Master's and Fellow's garden
6. bowling green

1882

1. First Court
2. chapel
3. library
4. Master's Lodge
5. Master's and Fellow's gardens
6. observatory
7. New Court

1980

1. First Court
2. chapel
3. library
4. Master's Lodge
5. Master's and Fellow's gardens
6. New Court

1997

1. First Court
2. chapel
3. library
4. Master's Lodge
5. Master's and Fellow's gardens
6. New Court

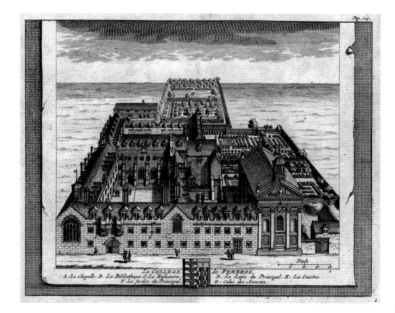

previous page: The new court buildings viewed from New Court created by Giles Gilbert Scott's college buildings of the 1880s. The site was occupied by private gardens and the 1920s lodge bounded by tall hedges and walls.

left: Sequence of plans chronicling changes to the site.

right: Early eighteenth century copy of David Loggan's 1682 view from the west illustrating Pembroke College.

opposite: The sundial, designed by the Cardozo Kindersley Workshop.

Thus, around the "First Court" (or Old Court, completed in the 1460s and hitherto much rebuilt) are still visible the chapel, hall, student rooms, kitchen and buttery, and the Master's Lodge. Significantly however, the notion of court implies complete enclosure, an aspect that is not borne out by the various instantiations at Pembroke: all of the courts have open sides, thereby establishing, on the one hand, an identifiable unit, while, on the other, creating a spatial link to the larger collective space.

Outwardly, the college appeared homogeneous, inwardly, the constituent parts were volumetrically and architecturally distinct. Subsequent extensions both along Trumpington Street (including Sir Christopher Wren's Chapel of 1665, his first completed building, extended by George Gilbert Scott Junior following his appointment in 1878 as architect to the college, succeeding Sir Alfred Waterhouse) and along Pembroke Street followed this pattern: Ivy Court and New Court (by George Gilbert Scott Junior, 1879–1883) completed the northern edge and formed a solid corner on the intersection of Pembroke Street and Tennis Court Road. Maurice Webb's Master's Lodge, 1933, in the southeastern corner, of necessity free-standing, was the first of the Pembroke College buildings to depart from the perimeter tradition, a break that was to be underlined by Marshall Sisson's dormitory building along the eastern boundary of the generous bowling green, Orchard Building, 1958, that was set back from Tennis Court Road, thereby breaking the tradition of building to the perimeter.

Given, in general, the colleges' unending need for further accommodation and the restriction on sites within the by now densely developed town fabric of Cambridge, and the particular intention on behalf of Pembroke in the mid-1980s to add nearly 100 student rooms, a fellow's set, a computer centre and various meeting rooms, the reflection of the College's history and the impact on the town's fabric had to be studied. Eric Parry was appointed in 1987 to conduct such an enquiry, defining the options that existed within the confines of Pembroke's property. His central recommendation, to demolish Webb's Master's Lodge in order to provide appropriate liberties for the large expansion, was accepted by the Master, Fellows and Scholars of Pembroke. The construction programme thus was enlarged to include a new Master's Lodge.

Interior view of the structurally glazed lantern which ventilates the corridors during the summer. Dichroic glass sculpture by Peter Aldridge.

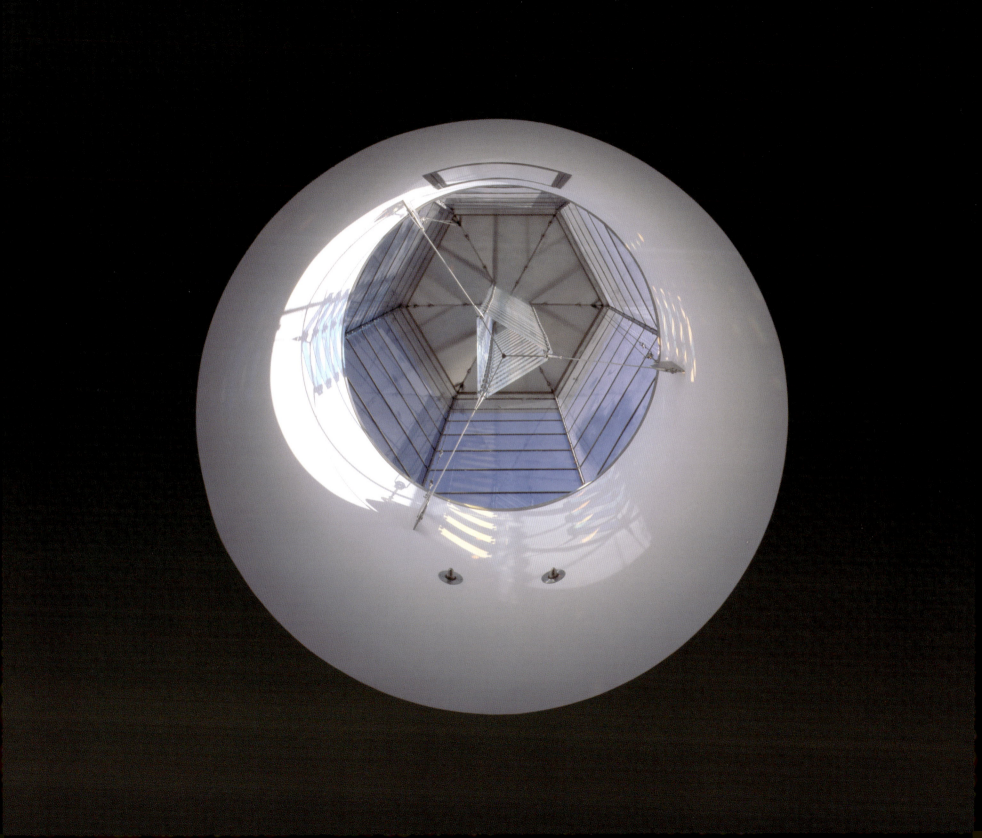

first floor: staggered party walls in the student rooms
swallow wardrobes and wash basins to both sides.

1. Fellow's flat
2. student common room
3. raised court
4. study bedrooms
5. kitchen
6. lodge reception room
7. domestic stair

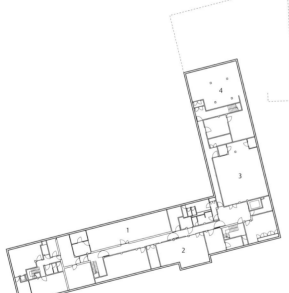

1:750

1:500

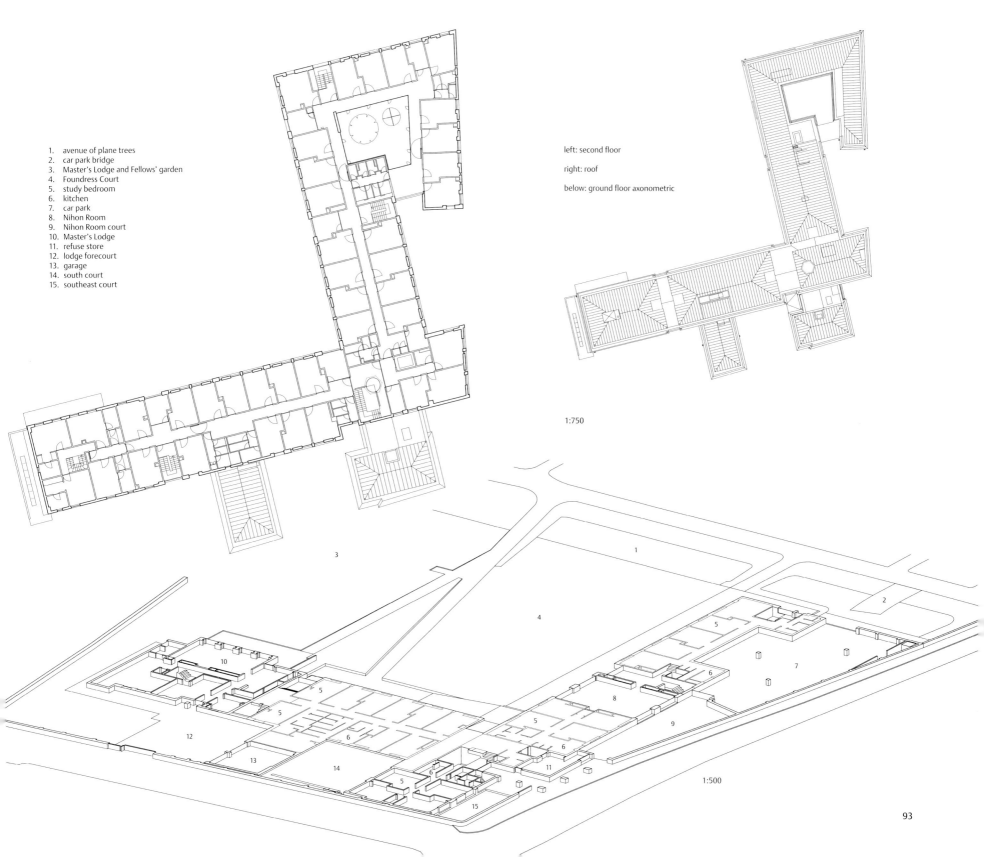

1. avenue of plane trees
2. car park bridge
3. Master's Lodge and Fellows' garden
4. Foundress Court
5. study bedroom
6. kitchen
7. car park
8. Nihon Room
9. Nihon Room court
10. Master's Lodge
11. refuse store
12. lodge forecourt
13. garage
14. south court
15. southeast court

left: second floor

right: roof

below: ground floor axonometric

1:750

1:500

93

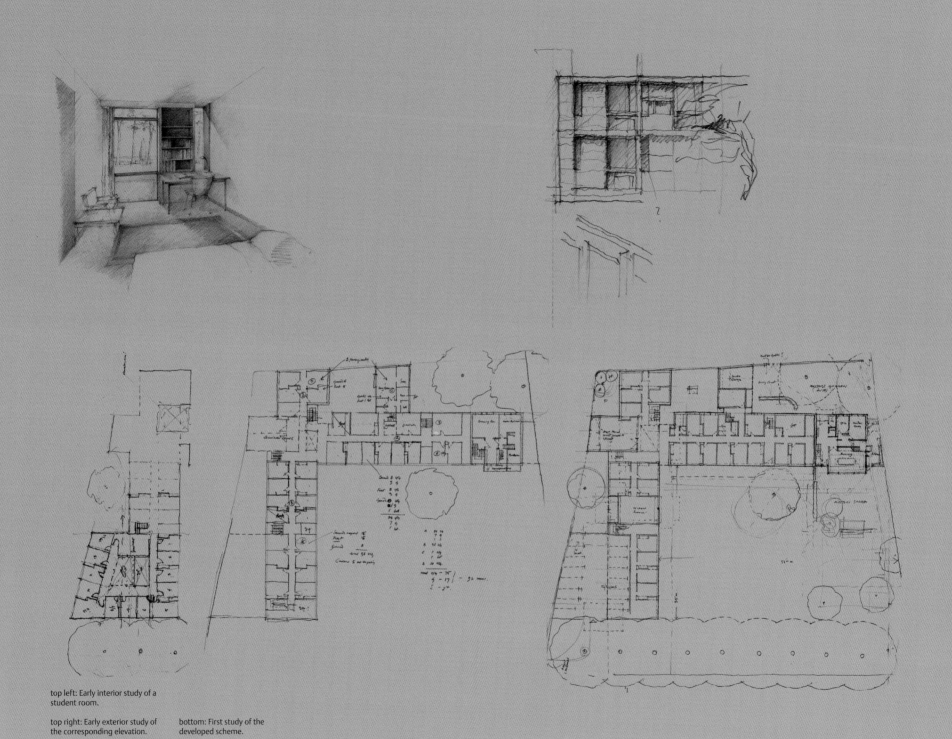

top left: Early interior study of a
student room.

top right: Early exterior study of
the corresponding elevation.

bottom: First study of the
developed scheme.

Stairwell in student
accommodation building.

left: View of west wing from New Court.

right: Detail of main entrance.

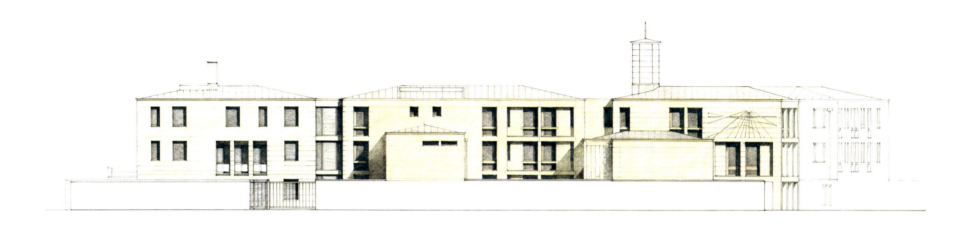

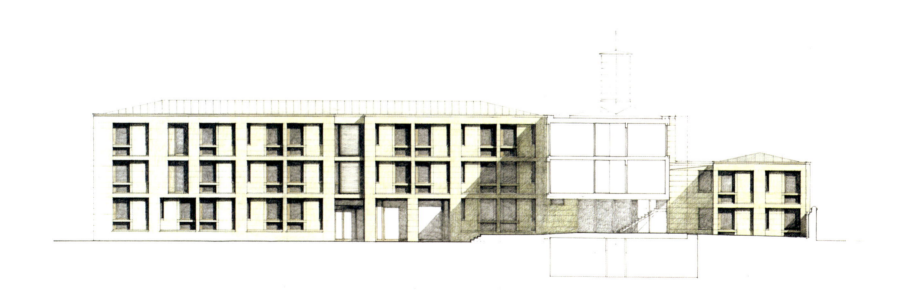

top: South elevation.

bottom: West elevation.

Eric Parry Architects' design for the new Foundress Court is a carefully balanced configuration, giving equal prominence to the addition's new public as well as private faces. Loosely speaking, the new contextual figure follows an articulated linear structure with two heads at either ends: that of the Master's Lodge and that of the northern reticulation of the students' rooms. The lateral wings provide for enclosures to smaller courts facing east and southwards across the College's boundaries. More significantly, these configurations, when seen in the context of the domestically-scaled street of Tennis Court Terrace and the institutionally fragmented street edge of Tennis Court Road, provide a dialectical response to the thesis of presencing the College to the public, the antithesis of wishing to respect the local inhabitants' concern for overscaled development, and the synthesis of nevertheless expressing a complex unity through the dominance of the new building's materiality.

Towards the private side, the new western and northern facades of Foundress Court create the same partially complete spatial definition as the other four courts, thereby underlining the collective quality of the Bowling Green. The masterplan by Eric Parry investigated the possibility of adding a third wing, as has been common in previous court developments, only to be confronted by the nineteenth century restrictive covenant between Pembroke and Peterhouse, prohibiting overlooking of adjacent properties. A west wing would have infringed that covenant.

In contrast to the quality of previous students' accommodation, the provision of gathering spaces, both internal and external, increases the identifiability of the new building. Given the fact that the rooms are aligned on double-loaded corridors, whose lengths are potentially alienating, regular articulations of these corridors by means of kitchens, hallways and stairwells, widening of the corridor, the common room and the raised court introduce differences and points of identification. To some designers of a ortho-rationalist mind, these 'aberrations' from the straight and narrow might appear all too picturesque in the pejorative sense. They are, of course, picturesque, understood in its proper phenomenological sense as defined by English landscape theorists, such as, for example, Uvedale Price.

Parry's design stands in the long tradition of institutions with a recognisable character, identifiable parts, responsiveness to site and programme. Within a coherent language Foundress Court expresses, as an educational institution, a high variety of differences. These are as readable in the treatment of the exterior as they are on the interior. Precedents such as Max Bill's Hochschule für Gestaltung at Ulm, 1950–1955, that is a reflection of Hannes Meyer's Trade Union School at Bernau, 1928–1930, which in turn owes its roots to the early enlightenment version by Thomas Jefferson's buildings around the "Lawn" for the University of Virginia, integrate residential components with teaching facilities in such a way as to establish both order through repetition as well as particularity through local inventions.

Master's Lodge forecourt.

1:330

East sectional elevation with raised court.

EPA's Foundress Court stands in this line of thinking and composition. The more ludic aspects of Le Corbusier's La Tourette facade system, theoretised further in John Weeks' explanations for Northwick Park Hospital, 1962–1964, in terms of an "Indeterminate Architecture", combines both a visually stimulating, differentiated exterior that conforms to both picturesque sensibilities as well as to the need to establish a grand order of familial tectonics. EPA's exterior architecture at Foundress Court is developed on more ordered lines: a regular grid is formed on most facades by the projecting Bath stone self-supporting tectonic frame against which more particular openings, resulting from the planimetric needs, are placed. Variations in the widths of the regular tectonic grid add a further nervous energy to the overall facade rhythm.

In considering the overall L-shaped development as a line with two ends and three side projections, the additive nature is subtly highlighted by the shallow pitched, hipped saddle roofs, a fact only visible from afar (as the projection of the parapets tend to obscure these), as well as by the stronger recesses with their larger glazing across the entrances. In this way, Parry has submitted the building to what appears as a calm order at first sight, an order which becomes richer and more reasoned as, through frequent observation, the eye follows the articulate stereotomy. The quality of the tectonic's skin is everywhere visible by the detailing of the joints, but especially at the entrance pieces, where the polyester powder coated cladding panel to the recessed rainwater pipe most certainly undercuts the impression of the grid's depth. Here, too, the

dialectic between image and fact enlightens the curious observer, an issue that can be identified in every detail of the stonework.

Facing the raised interior court at the northern end, an extensive glazed skin and glass panelled sanitary units indicate a conceptual rupture, one that introduces flush contemporary detailing to a masonry building. It is a gesture making simultaneously transparent the interior as well as reducing the configurational impact of the double-loaded corridor in its end section towards Tennis Court Road. What becomes visible there is a single bay with its end units off the inner gallery. This sleight of hand is as important as the reduction in height of the two southern wings and the manipulation of the eastern wings altogether: they are compositional techniques to reduce the impact of a new, large institution. Analogously, Philip Dowson of Arup Associates reduced the visual impact of the overall development by reducing widths of the end units of the Sir Thomas White Quadrangle at St John's College, Oxford, 1970–1975, while clearly defining the vertical circulation and exoskeletal structure, emphases already explored by Louis Kahn for the AN Richards Medical Research Laboratories at the University of Pennsylvania, 1957–1961, in Philadelphia. The degrees of differences in the identification of each residential or laboratory unit are instructive in so far as these considerations are fundamental to the structural order of the respective repetitive units. Furthermore, the changes in thermal insulation legislation has rendered those structural solutions impossible that offer thermal bridges. The tectonic grid on the facades of EPA's Foundress Court therefore symbolises the interior subdivisions.

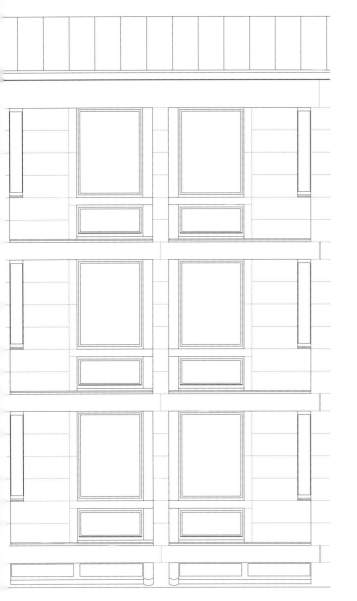

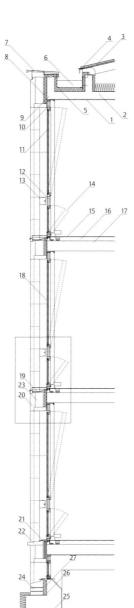

1:75

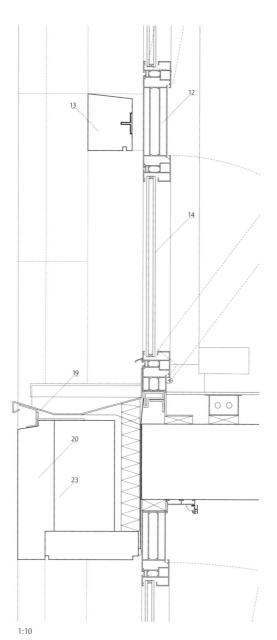

1:10

1. 12 mm plaster with paint finish
2. 150 mm concrete roof slab
3. treated sw boarding
4. roof covering of pre-patinated zinc
5. rigid insulation laid to falls
6. inset gutter
7. polyester powder coated aluminium coping, secret fixed
8. liquid applied bituminous membrane
9. fascia fixed through 75 mm insulation to 150 mm concrete upstand
10. polyester powder coated extruded aluminium edge trim
11. side tilt/turn inward-opening polyester powder coated aluminium double-glazed window, thermally broken
12. thermally broken trickle ventilator
13. 150 x 150 mm solid stone transom
14. bottom pivot inward opening etched glazed unit
15. carpet floor finish
16. 80 mm screed
17. 200 mm concrete floor slab
18. polyester powder coated aluminium double-glazed window, thermally broken
19. polyester powder coated aluminium gutter connected to concealed rwp, gutter flange bolted to precast lintel
20. 3250 x 100 mm thick Bath
&   stone fascia and soffit
23. backed with precast concrete lintel, fixed with restraint fixings to floor slab
21. polyester powder coated window sill
22. profiled stone sill
24. engineering brick plinth
25. concrete basement retaining wall
26. dpc
27. 50 mm insulation

100

1. self-supporting Bath stone outer leaf
2. inner blockwork panel
3. slot window
4. bookshelves
5. full height aluminium window panel, lower panel translucent glazing, accessible for cleaning from the interior
6. curtain collects over secret gutter drainage discharge pipe
7. timber shutter
8. medicine cabinet
9. wash basin
10. wardrobe
11. entrance door
12. oak boarding
13. bedroom dimensions determined to allow alternative location for bed
14. desk designed not to block light from lower window panel
15. radiator

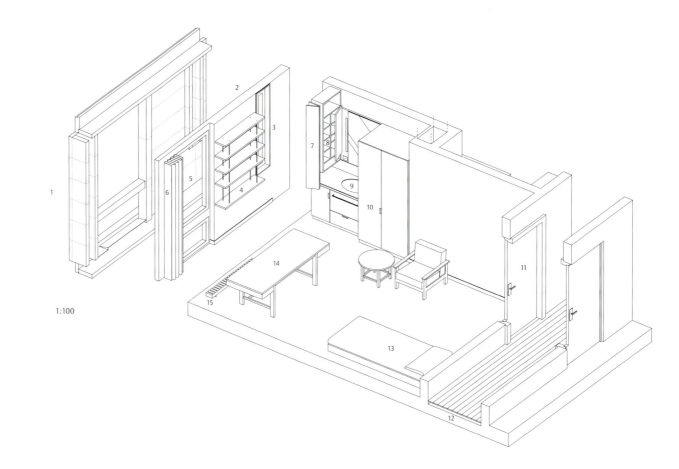

1:100

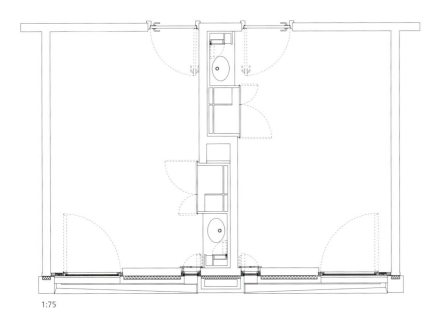

1:75

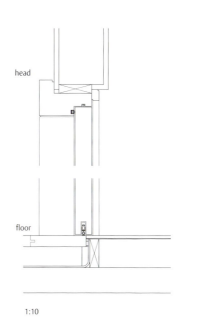

head

floor

1:10

left: Plan showing back to back room configuration.

right: Details as shown.

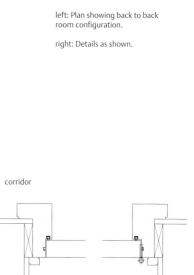

corridor

room

101

Tennis Court Road facade detail.

Each room has a recessed assembly of a wardrobe and a washbasin. Two windows, one large and one narrow, allow for varied ventilation and lighting, the furniture designed by the office is plain while also referring to College traditions of robustness and comfort. The rooms are dimensioned so that a range of layouts are possible. Other details for the stairs or the interior finishes of the Nihon Room demonstrate the architects' skill in bringing precision and care to an institutional type that conventionally receives little attention at these levels. The equally well-considered Master's Lodge can be seen as an echo to the smooth northeastern corner. In its garden facade, the lodge recalls Georgian houses with their metal awnings over the *piano nobile* balconies, their spare detailing and laconic but imposing materiality. The programme asked for the inclusion within the confines of the house of further bedrooms, a request that the practice accommodated by aligning two units on the eastern side of the stairway. On the interior, the dining room takes full advantage of the Lodge's location by allowing views north and south of the site, thereby bringing the overall composition to a suitable termination.

Foundress Court, given its privileged position within a wealthy institution, is a rare example of dignified housing of the late 1990s. Housing for the public was no longer a continuing discourse in a country that was once the origin of much speculation in the positive as well as negative sense, but a country always at the forefront of housing research. Luxury apartments in the manner of warehouse conversions to lofts, the ever popular single family and semi-detached houses in new suburbia (whether on the edges of cities or on recouped brown field sites) and the conversion of unrented office space into apartment units were the major areas of housing production under late Thatcherism. EPA's design at Pembroke is different in so far as it is neither historicist nor devoid of links to the local traditions, Foundress Court is consciously ambiguous: it establishes its own identifiable physical and typological presence while at the same time being part of the existing College fabric.

Apart from three bays, which define a minor entrance, the east facade is expressed as a boundary wall with deeply incised openings.

103

Agace Residence
London

The house is one of a listed terrace of houses, a complete and elegantly proportioned late Georgian remnant in Islington, London. These houses have tended to return to single ownerships from post-war multi-tenanted use. This house had a separate lower ground flat hemmed in by a retaining wall to the rear garden and by a relatively generous 'area' to the street. The intervention, because in this case there has been no increase in volume or area, was about the reinvention of the rear of the building to accommodate uses for the pattern of family life.

opposite left: Plan at X–X'.

opposite right: Terrace with shower room and received ventilation panel. Double-height window with pivoting ground floor door open.

On the lower ground floor, with the removal of the central spine wall and the rear wall at this level the space runs from the front court to the back court to act as a day room for the young family. The composition seen from the garden was conceived as a set of abstracted rectangular planes that can be adjusted to reflect diurnal and seasonal patterns of use. The static element is the suspended opaque glass box, a reinterpretation of the 'privvy'—here a top-lit shower room, the floor of which is a stainless steel tray with hardwood duckboards. The sloping glass connects to the sill of the original stairway fanlight. This box cantilevers a little to form a canopy to the glazed door leading from the internal stair landing, with its balcony overlooking the dayroom below, and the external terrace landing leading to the garden. The large tripartite glass window—echoing the proportions of a Georgian sash—can be read sinking or rising from the excavated lower garden court. It is a day/night shadow box resolved open during the summer and closed during the winter. The vertical gap between the floating ablutions box and the shadow box is taken up by solid opening panels the upper for ventilation, the lower a door between the day room and the court.

1. new court excavated in rear garden
2. terrace to door from stair landing
3. internal balcony
4. recess to receive solid ventilation panel
5. recess to receive side door
6. family room and double-height south facing space connecting to living room
7. living room
8. opaque glass walled shower and toilet top lit with glazed ventilating panel in flank wall
9. existing clerestory light to main stair
10. main stair
11. utility room

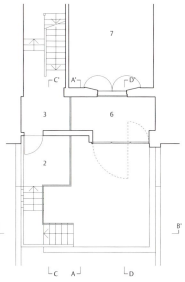

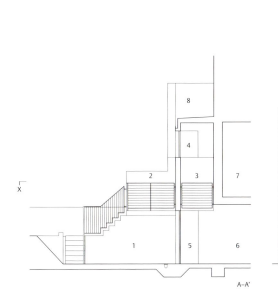

A–A'

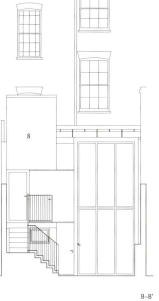

B–B'

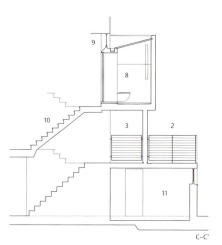

C–C'

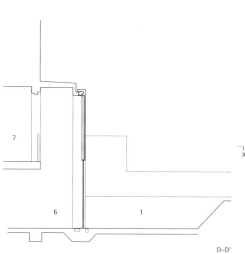

D–D'

Damai Suria
Kuala Lumpur
Malaysia

Malaysia in general, and Kuala Lumpur in particular, have been the recipients of much international investment in Southeast Asia during the early 1990s, mobilising internal and external forces with considerable symbolic pretensions as the world's tallest high-rise, the Petronas Twin Towers, 1998, by Cesar Pelli, have shown. Imported from the USA, the type of urban development encompassing a complex of offices surrounded by an enormous commercial base complete with a public park above an underground car park has proven to be an attractive mix for the revival of the inner city, filling

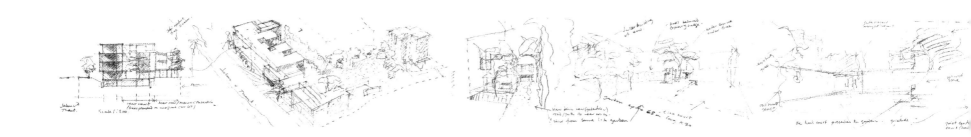

As with any city, Kuala Lumpur's urban development and architecture give enough indications as to the city's different organisational logics. Colonial infrastructure and governing buildings with the early British colonial shop-houses that defined the original street fabric still act as a backbone to the continuing reinvention of urbanity by each subsequent generation. The 1990s mixture of high-rise apartment blocks set within a hardly identifiable curtilage together with the glamourous and guilded links of international hotel chains in the downtown area, standing besides low-rise concrete developments of the 1950s results in extraordinary scalar disjunctions. The incongruous public space and the complete exposure to the unrelenting sunshine in parts of this new metropolis stand in marked contrast to the edges of the inner city that engage with the undulating verdant topography. Here, on Kuala Lumpur's periphery, the slightly more cohesive realisation of low-rise units on separate lots known as *kampongs* or compounds—gated communities—has been a Malay tradition. Eric Parry Architects was commissioned by an enterprising developer to design an unusual, multi-storey version of such a *kampong* on an L-shaped corner plot in one of the most desirable neighbourhoods of Kuala Lumpur. The reaction to the disjunctions in the nearby inner city, the introverted character of the gated communities set the context for the design critique.

Many of the clashes in scale between the urban growth of centuries and the sudden change in scalar force of international investment are noticeable, but some of these are ameliorated by the fecund vegetation sprouting in the interstices, and providing the much needed natural shading in this tropical climate (temperatures around 30 degrees centigrade, above 90 per cent humidity, and frequent downpours). Nature's principle—to create layers of ventilated space—has been adopted in vernacular architecture and in recent buildings by observant designers, most notably by the architects of the Kuala Lumpur General Hospital (Wells & Joyce, competition of 1961). This complex of wards, operating theatres, outpatients departments, and residential quarters for the staff are grouped into collective orthogonal complexes, which in turn are held together by narrow pedestrian covered footpaths. Each collective complex is expressed with slightly different physiognomies, all stemming from a genotypical base of forms. The principle of layered spaces, screens, loggias and covered walkways provides an architectural version of vegetal solar protection. Cross-ventilation within these shaded space segments provides a form of insulation generating a relative temperature difference that allows occupants to feel more comfortable. This principle, together with the compositional concerns, was an inspiration for this housing scheme.

previous page: Damai Suria streetside at the corner of the Jalan U Thant, heading away from downtown Kuala Lumpur to the right, and Ampang Hilir to the left. Weather is less seasonal than wet or dry, here a characteristic moody moment between a squall and a downpour.

top: First thoughts sketches faxed to the client on day one. Whilst the design evolved in London, during the later working drawing and tender phases Nick Jackson moved to Malaysia and with our colleague and former collaborator Chris Wong and his firm C'Arch Archictecture + Design. As a result a 24 hour office was born.

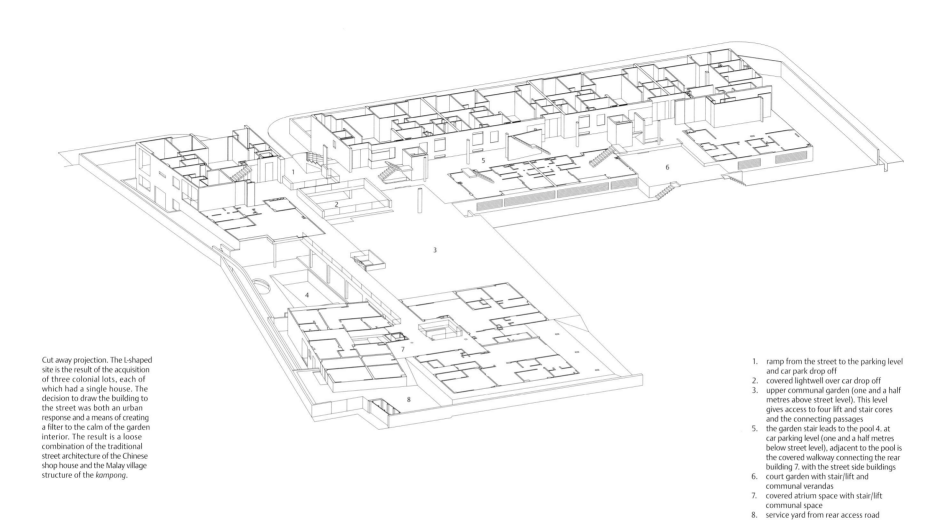

Cut away projection. The L-shaped site is the result of the acquisition of three colonial lots, each of which had a single house. The decision to draw the building to the street was both an urban response and a means of creating a filter to the calm of the garden interior. The result is a loose combination of the traditional street architecture of the Chinese shop house and the Malay village structure of the *kampong*.

1. ramp from the street to the parking level and car park drop off
2. covered lightwell over car drop off
3. upper communal garden (one and a half metres above street level). This level gives access to four lift and stair cores and the connecting passages
4. the garden stair leads to the pool 4. at car parking level (one and a half metres below street level), adjacent to the pool is the covered walkway connecting the rear building 7. with the street side buildings
5. court garden with stair/lift and communal verandas
6. covered atrium space with stair/lift communal space
7. service yard from rear access road

112

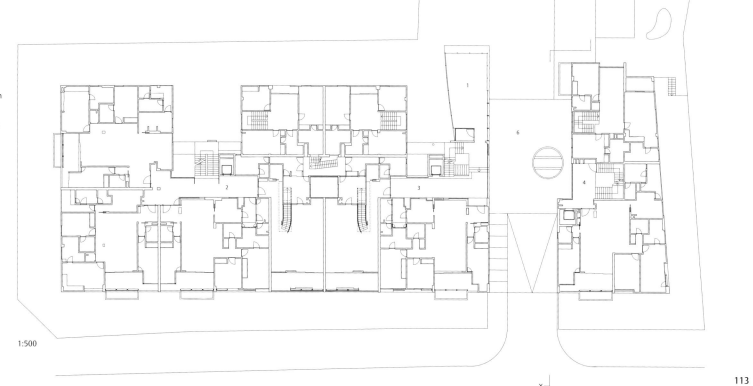

X'⌐

opposite: Early site plan with
entrance court and access to
car park by separate ramp.

right: First floor.
The apartments range in size from
186 m square to 465 m square.

1. communal room overlooking
   the central garden
2–5. the continuous passages of
   the ground floor level now
   become naturally ventilated
   covered hallways and
   communal areas around
   the far stair and lift cores
6. roof over car drop off two
   floors below, and passages
   at ground level

1:500

X⌐

EPA's interest in ecological aspects of contemporary construction was nurtured in projects such as the Sussex Innovation Centre, in which low technological and passive systems were used for a flexible laboratory and office building to achieve a low energy building. The Innovation Centre was organised as a linear, double-loaded corridor building for constructional, contextual and ecological reasons. In the case of the Kuala Lumpur housing compound, an expanded version of the linear type was developed, on this occasion along a double-loaded openly ventilated corridor together with a secondary block set into the back of the site and connected by a covered walkway.

Comparing this configuration for Damai Suria with Pembroke College, the general contextual response in the former demonstrates an affirmative urban character: implied hard and continuous, coplanar facades towards the road—Jalan U-Thant—and a clear corner towards Pesiarian Ampang Hilir. The secondary articulations within this facade such as balconies, overhanging eaves, recesses, loggias, and triple-height entrance porch create a welcome counterpoint to the otherwise simple planar gesture. Furthermore, the constructional and material details such as the reflective glass balustrades, the sliding and operable louvres complete the overall diversity within an ultimately bold statement. This attitude of counterpointing a clear formal gesture with different orders of articulation creates a secondary form of the picturesque, an underlying sensibility that can be sensed at Damai Suria throughout. For instance,

the composition of the entrance porch: where a generous external arrival hall, protected from rain and sun by two overlapping terraces or roofs with a variety of openings that filter light to an agreeable level has been created. As most residents and their guests arrive by car, there is an appropriate and contemporary welcome at the ramped lower ground floor, bounded at the rear by a wall of falling water that is set back sufficiently to give a glancing view of the small swimming pool beyond. Contrary to many underground car parks that are afflicted by engine fumes and other smells, the design has achieved a unique equality between pedestrians and car drivers that is at once relaxed and grand. Such a synthesis of opposites has been made possible through the delicate choice of materials and details, discreet steel handrails and clear glass balustrades, pebbled terraces as a hard version of the pervasive landscaping that passes through the external areas and a firm definition of spaces through the precise setting of dimensions and proportions.

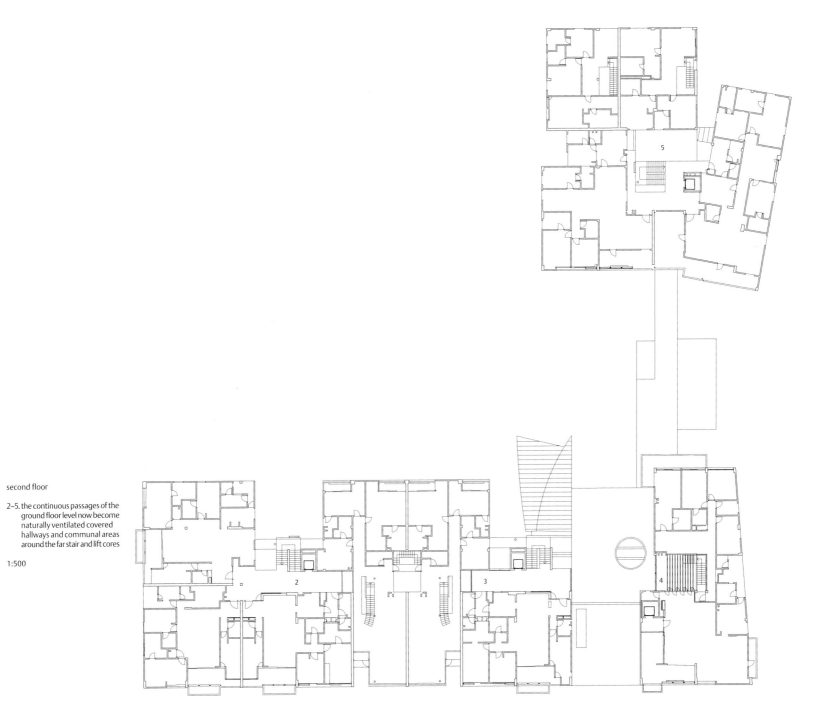

second floor

2–5. the continuous passages of the
ground floor level now become
naturally ventilated covered
hallways and communal areas
around the far stair and lift cores

1:500

all visitors
please
report to
security
staff

left: View from street level to entrance showing car ramp leading down to the basement parking, with pedestrian bridge link to apartments on each side and pedestrian stepped ramp in the entrance.

below: Detail of retaining wall and granite water wall, adjacent to gate with pool beyond.

opposite left: View of rear apartment building from the garden. The framed louvred panels can be parted to open the verandah or closed completely.

opposite right: Early facade study with louvres in local hardwood. The verandas open directly to the reception rooms. In plan the reception space and dining space are contiguous so as to allow natural ventilation and fan aided air movement through the apartment.

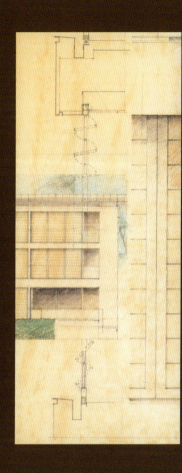

left: Communal garden to the right with canopies and passages at four levels over the entrance. Left duplex apartment with pool below with large apartment on one level above.

opposite top: Street elevation.

opposite centre: Garden elevation.

opposite bottom:
Section through entrance.

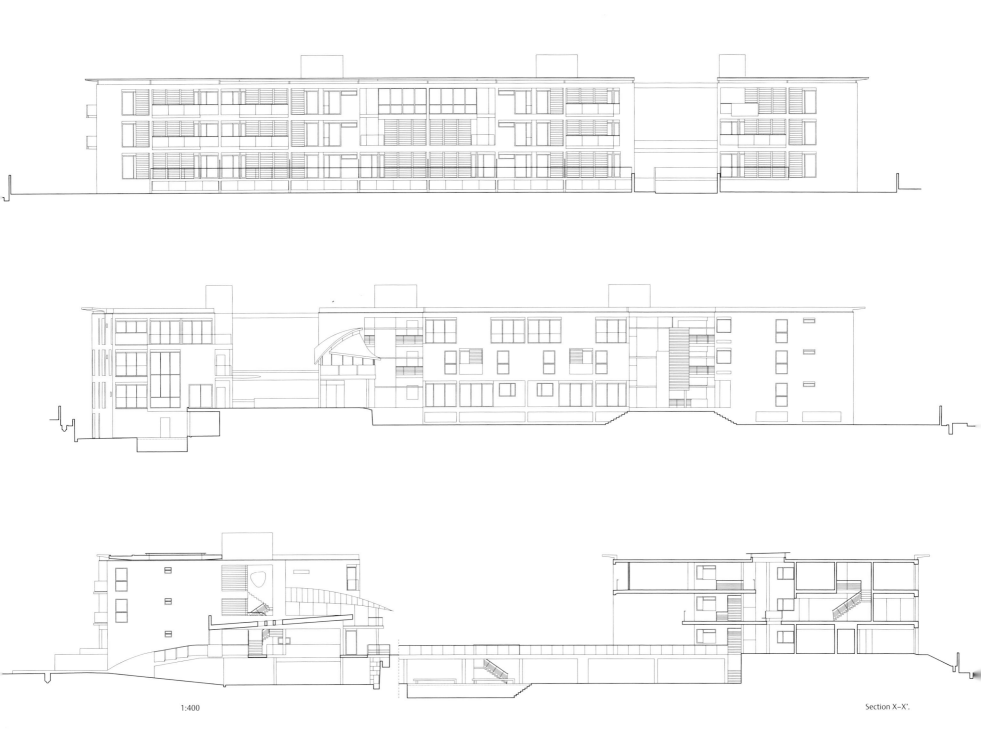

1:400

Section X–X'.

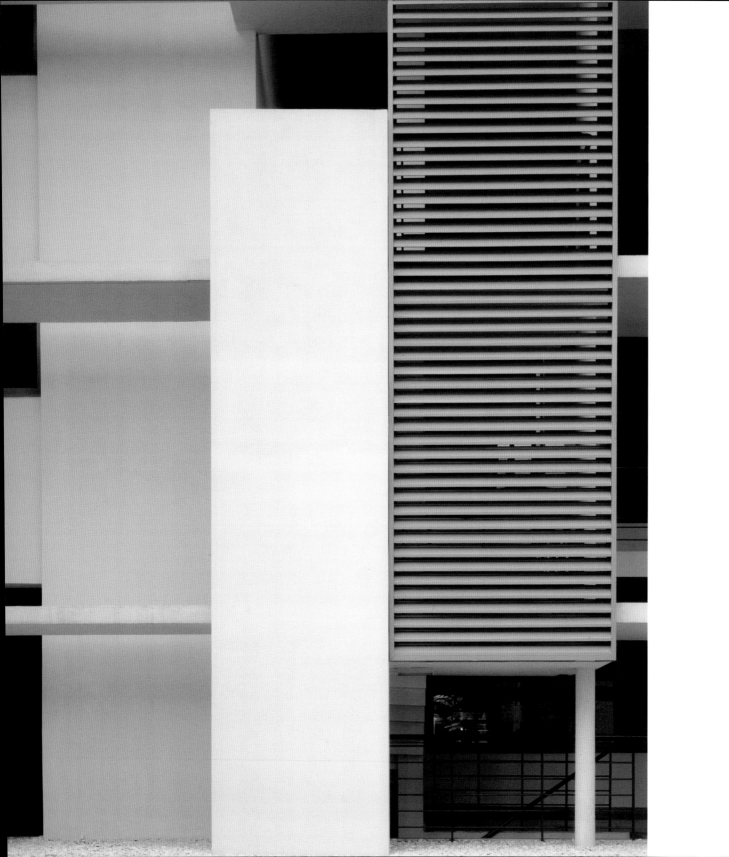

Contrary to Pembroke College, EPA have created an articulated inner realm in which one north-, one east- and one west-facing block, together form a communal club house along its external corridor, bound to the garden in a variety of ways. Even the south-facing elevation of the rear building is broken in its planar presence by the shift in the eastern wing, which is aligned to follow the site line. Thus, in comparing Pembroke College to Damai Suria, the skill in the development of configurations becomes evident, it is a skill that shapes a specific response to answer a given and quite distinct situation, even though superficially the configurations might appear similar in both cases. Most importantly, clear logic and highly localised differentiations are used in masterful balance, as the relation between corridor and garden courts shows. There is in this architecture always sufficient repetition and equally sufficient variation to create an underlying order, which is given a local anchor, an element of identifiability that the vast majority of architects are unable to achieve. The sense of order is mature, precise, knowing. This understanding is applied right up to the layout and detailing of the apartments. Entrance lobby, living room and threshold to the bedrooms are carefully calibrated and articulated in a synthesis of neo-Plastic diction and traditional spatial syntax befitting haute-bourgeois life styles.

In combination with the smaller and larger vegetation, it is possible to see the interstitial elements of the housing complex as hard landscape, an in-between version that deflects light and gives shade. During the day, this interpretation might seem a bit far fetched, during the night, when indirect artificial light softly reflects from the concrete walls through the various louvers and balustrades, allowing the terraces, steps and elevated floors to appear as if they were floating, this line of reading and thinking becomes more credible. When understood in relation to the lessons that EPA have learnt from Malaysia's botany, vernacular and historical architecture, it is an impressive direction in which contemporary efforts in developing a more ecologically sound architecture might move.

left: View of the open club room over communal garden.

right: Preliminary sketches showing canted entrance canopy to reduce shadow in perspective and to emphasise the opening to the garden. Also showing the development of the geometry of the club room roof.

Taylor Residence
London

Densely developed, Knightsbridge contains both monumental squares as well as tiny alleys and passages hidden from general public view. This house belongs to that category of secret urban spaces that are the subject of London's myths, the ideal of film scouts.

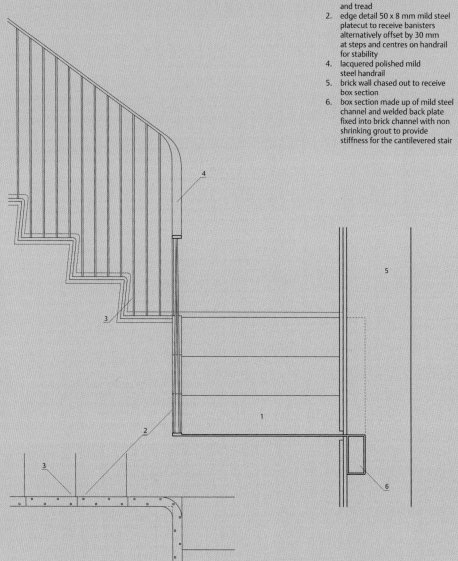

elevation of stairwell looking towards
blank party wall

1. hallway and cloak
2. bedrooms, laundry
3. living room
4. bedroom
5. adjoining roof
6. stressed skin steel landing
7. roof terrace
8. double-glazed glass roof
    and glass beams

stair detail

1. 8 mm mild steel sheet riser
    and tread
2. edge detail 50 x 8 mm mild steel
    platecut to receive banisters
    alternatively offset by 30 mm
    at steps and centres on handrail
    for stability
4. lacquered polished mild
    steel handrail
5. brick wall chased out to receive
    box section
6. box section made up of mild steel
    channel and welded back plate
    fixed into brick channel with non
    shrinking grout to provide
    stiffness for the cantilevered stair

1:75

1:20

Approached from a narrow street lined with two-storey terraced houses, the passage leads to the residual sites to the rear of large late Georgian family houses. Originally the L-shaped configuration was a series of additions and alterations that contained two interlocking maisonettes, which were vertically connected via four independently located flights of stairs. The current owners, a family with two children, and an interest in contemporary art, commissioned Eric Parry Architects to merge the two units into a single house. The result is a clear distribution of rooms off a centralised, top-lit staircase located at the fulcrum of the L. Full advantage was thereby taken of the strategic location for the most efficient and minimal circulation system while also using the tower-like nature of the stairwell to bring daylight onto the ground floor of the house, previously a dark and cramped space. Much of the wall surface of the lightwell is now extensively used for the family's art collection.

Cleaning the adjoining rooms in preparation for a large kitchen at ground level and a large living room at first floor level immediately provided the generosity that the original two units lacked. By the judicious removal and addition of new partitions, the remaining floors were altered to accommodate bedrooms and studies.

The staircase was the practice's main intervention. Structurally a three-dimensional interlocking of folded steel treads and triangulated balustrading, the presence of the new staircase exudes the spirit of the minimal, with the handrailing continues the Georgian tradition of effortless crafting of smooth, highly complex three-dimensional profiles.

top: Exploded axonometric showing the stacked configuration of the four floors. A four-storey stair void was made into the heel of the boot shaped plan of the building leading directly from the hallway (from the courtyard) and to the upper central master bedroom floor and roof garden.

1. court
2. hall
3. kitchen dining
4. independent flat
5. bedroom
6. reception
7. bedroom suite
8. terrace

opposite: View into the courtyard reached from a mews passage. The site, deeply embedded in a labyrinthian knot of urban fabric, gave rise to the L-shaped aspect configuration into the secluded courtyard. The larger of the two wings had been rebuilt in the 1930s as a pair of stacked maisonettes with a common entrance position at the internal angle of the wings. An inefficient low strength concrete frame created a five bay single span in juxtaposition to the early nineteenth century three-storey wing.

Public Space and Southwark
Tourist Information Centre
London

Immediately after the exhibition "Future Southwark" held in a disused car wash in June–July 1996 on ways of improving urban design and architectural deficits within Southwark, the London borough commissioned Eric Parry Architects to address the area for which the office had already undertaken numerous design investigations: the footings and on-ramps of London Bridge as well as Duke Hill and Tooley Street. These three intensively used public routes presented a combination of neglect and abuse still common to much of London today.

previous page: View from the roof of the adjacent office building to the new public space at the foot of London Bridge. This was the vantage point from which we video recorded the activity within the area for analysis before developing our proposals.

top: Photo collage of the site before the interventions. To the left, London Bridge and to the right Duke Hill Street. The concrete balustrade to the ramp leading to London Bridge Station acts as a defensive wall insulating commuters from the 'Borough'. The Corporation of London owns the land of differentiated paving at the centre of the image, Southwark own the rest. This is a political no-man's land as the Corporation seeks to reduce the public realm by developing the site and Southwark, the planning authority, have refused to grant permission. The brick wall is a non-structural cosmetic in front of the upper section of a retaining wall. The continuous railings made this a confusing place.

bottom: The historic level of Tooley Street underneath the ramp, the one remaining arch of John Rennies bridge, 1831, visible to the right.

London Bridge and the City skyline beyond, in 1616. Detail from Claes Jan Visseler's etching. The threshold to London from Roman times marked by the traitors' heads above the southern gate has evolved into highway engineering and crowd control.

The sole element of continuity in this confluence of vehicular and pedestrian paths was the road surface. Everything else had to make do with the rough and ready of centuries of embankment engineering, post-war make-shift adaptations, cosmetic obscuring of the rupture due to the sale of the old bridge. From nearby London Bridge Railway Station 2.6 million commuters pass across these surfaces every day. Looking at the images of the state prior to Eric Parry Architects' interventions, one wonders how the public and their political representatives have been able to ignore such conditions for so long. One explanation seems to be that one of the qualities of human nature is its ability to become accustomed to even the worst situation given sufficient time, the other is that the site is a boundary between the ownership of Southwark and the Corporation of London.

The Southwark Initiative, initiated by Fred Manson, head of Regeneration at Southwark, then sought finally to improve key areas with a modest budget of 3.65 million pounds. Other architects chosen to participate included Pierre d'Avoine, Muf, Patel Taylor, East Architects, and Caruso St John. EPA's proposal next to London Bridge Railway Station is at once radical as it is a sympathetic interpretation of the gritty character of the dense Victorian fabric. The primary focus was to give greater care to the spatial impressions and sense of orientation of pedestrians. The different levels of the three surrounding streets, the typical modernist-autistic attempts to negotiate these changes in levels by concrete encased stairs and ramps, the lack of activities at key intersections of paths, the general dimensional meanness of the public space, all these were issues that the design redressed.

Tooley Street, located six m below the bridge and running beneath the one remaining vault of the old London Bridge, rises slightly towards its eastern end to meet the eastwards falling Duke Street Hill. Thus, like a triangular coil, the rotational pavements from the lowest to the highest levels have been resurfaced in traditional York Stone, and in combinations of exposed aggregate concrete panels that are laid on a palim in some instances on the more generous northern side of Duke Street Hill pavement with asphalt so as to accommodate the flotsam-like arrangements of curvilinear stainless steel benches amongst the existing trees. The spatial clarity of the area has also been achieved thanks to the partial demolition of a concrete ramp/balustrade and the reshaping of the corner of the street junction, both seemingly obvious and simple measures, but both requiring considerable efforts at bureaucratic levels.

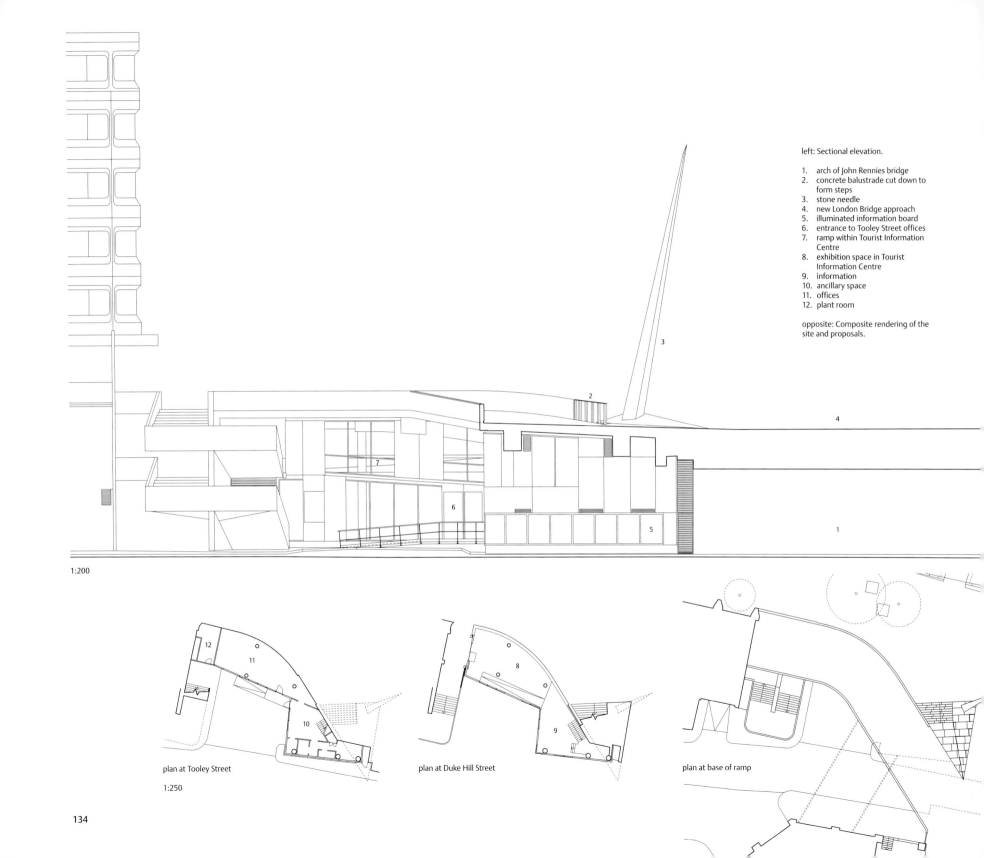

left: Sectional elevation.

1. arch of John Rennies bridge
2. concrete balustrade cut down to form steps
3. stone needle
4. new London Bridge approach
5. illuminated information board
6. entrance to Tooley Street offices
7. ramp within Tourist Information Centre
8. exhibition space in Tourist Information Centre
9. information
10. ancillary space
11. offices
12. plant room

opposite: Composite rendering of the site and proposals.

1:200

plan at Tooley Street

1:250

plan at Duke Hill Street

plan at base of ramp

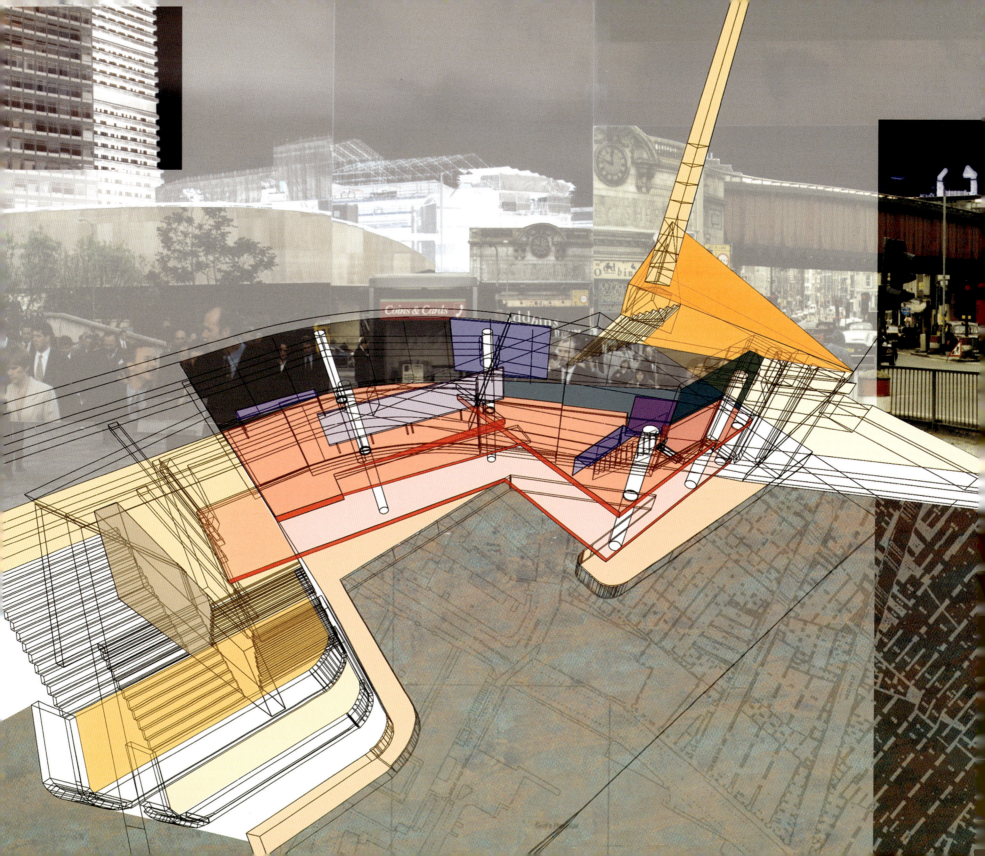

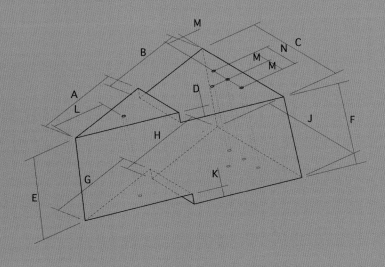

STONE REFERENCE NO.	TOP DIMENSIONS				STONE HEIGHT		BOTTOM DIMENSIONS			
	A	B	C	D	E	F	G	H	J	K
2	752.96	756.35	1118	75	600	600	781.75	785.15		75
3	725.86	729.25	1072.2	75	600	600	752.96	756.35	1118	75
4	698.76	702.15	1026.4	75	600	600	725.86	729.25	1072.2	75
5	671.66	675.05	980.6	75	600	600	698.76	702.15	1026.4	75
6	644.56	647.95	934.8	75	600	600	671.66	675.05	980.6	75
7	617.46	620.85	889	75	600	600	644.56	647.75	934.8	75
8	690.36	693.75	843.2	75	600	600	617.46	620.85	889	75
9	563.25	566.65	797.4	75	600	600	690.36	693.95	843.2	75
10	536.16	539.55	751.6	75	600	600	563.26	566.65	797.4	75
11	509.06	512.45	705.8	75	600	600	536.16	539.55	751.6	75
12	481.96	485.35	660	75	600	600	509.06	512.45	705.8	75
13	454.86	458.25	614.2	75	600	600	481.96	485.35	660	75
14	427.76	431.15	568.4	75	600	600	454.86	958.25	614.2	75
15	400.66	404.05	522.6	75	600	600	427.76	431.15	568.4	75
16	373.56	376.95	476.8	75	600	600	400.66	404.05	522.6	75
17	346.46	349.85	431	75	600	600	373.56	376.95	476.8	75
18	319.36	322.75	385.2	75	600	600	346.46	349.85	431	75
19	292.26	295.65	339.4	75	600	600	319.36	322.75	385.2	75
20	265.16	268.55	293.6	75	600	600	292.26	295.65	339.4	75
21	238.06	241.45	247.8	75	600	600	265.16	268.55	293.6	75
22	210.96	214.35	202	75	600	600	238.06	241.45	247.8	75
23	183.86	187.25	156.2	75	600	600	210.96	214.35	202.45	75
24	156.76	160.15	110.4	75	600	600	183.86	187.25	156.2	75

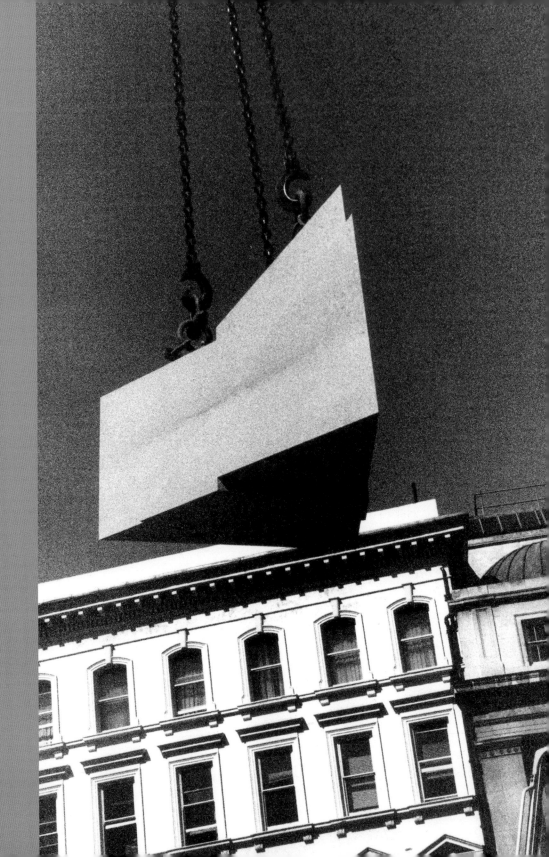

opposite left: Cutting schedule for one of the 25 stone blocks that make up the needle. The blocks are post-tensioned with threaded stainless steel rods. The stepped joint was derived from eighteenth century stereometric masonry and, in particular, the stone keys of the end bays of the colonnade to the Grand Theatre, Bordeaux, 1780, by Victor Louis.

opposite right: Block being lowered into place.

left: Elevation analysis of the performance of each joint under different loading conditions was carried out by Adams Kara Taylor, Structural Engineers. The stone was Portland Whitbed and a lime mortar was used to allow some flexibility and to ensure an evenly distributed load.

right: The needle under construction, by Ketton Masonry. To the right is the frame for the radiused glass to the Tourist Information Centre.

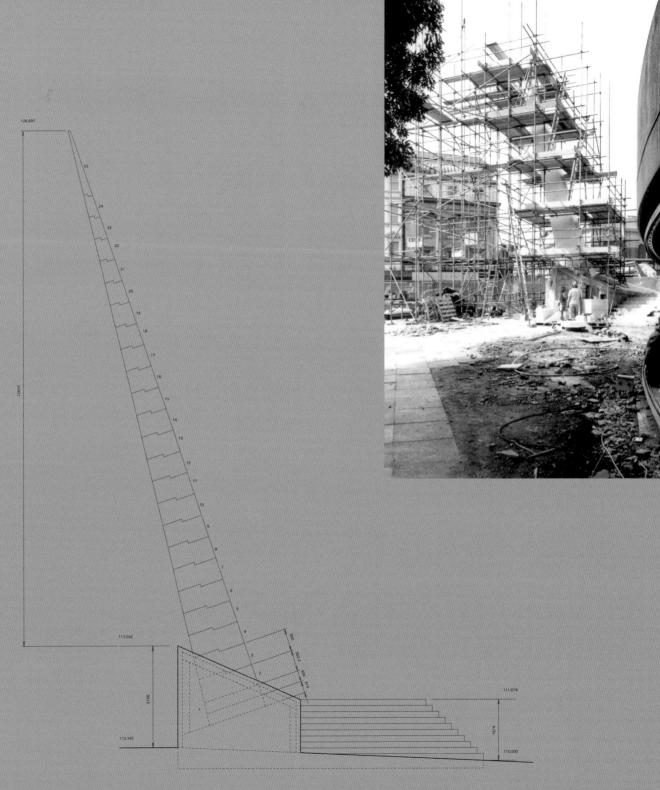

At the most crucial and voided intersection of the different levels, a new Tourist Information Centre has been built to act as an almost natural programmatic and architectural facility to collect the forces of pedestrian flow and to provide a much needed service at this self-evident location. Indeed, it was only after the analysis of a 24 hour video recording that the need for an information point at the corner of the bridge and Duke Street Hill was understood. Coincidentally, the results of a Southwark Borough study also concluded that this junction was the ideal spot for a tourist and information centre. Small exhibitions serving locals and tourists as well as a souvenir and bookshop complete the programme. At night, the Information Centre, which is subtly tucked into the underside of a ramp leading to the adjacent Colechurch House, lights the pavement.

The spatial composition of the Tourist Centre owes much to its given geometric condition with the ramping and curving surfaces. In addition to this, some of the spatial aesthetic can be related to two sources: Zaha Hadid and Alvaro Siza. Hadid's Weil Pavilions come to mind as well as Siza's banks in Oliveira de Azemeis and Vila do Conde. Whereas these examples are all free-standing, EPA's Tourist Centre is discovered by passing by it. The passage through and past it can be read as a conscious exposition of the warren-like character of the quarter's vaults, arcades, undercrofts, passages and embankments using contemporary materials. It is as if the cinematographic world of David Lynch had met Dickensian London through layers of panoramatic vitrines.

Topping all of this is the threateningly angled stone needle at the junction of London Bridge and Duke Street Hill. Constructed of joggle-jointed massive Portland Whitbed stone, internally secured with post-tensioned stainless steel rods, the needle of stone immediately recalls in the minds of Londoners the spoil of the Napoleonic War sited across on the northern riverside, on Victoria Embankment, the Egyptian obelisk called Cleopatra's Needle. Both

are relatively small objects, however, given their exposed setting, they have indelibly marked the location on which they stand. The triangular cross-section of the needle removes the shape from an all too direct lineage with the Egyptian obelisk. Together with the inclination, the needle bridges the iconographies of the ancient and the Constructivist domains. Added to that EPA's meticulous concern for craftsmanship, which in itself fuses the worlds of traditional masonry with that of advanced engineering, the Southwark needle exemplifies an inclusive historical dialectic, explicitly rejecting the 'secessionist' high-tech as well as blinkered classicism, to refer to extremes in contemporary British architecture.

Together then, the ramping Tourist Centre, the inclined needle and the resurfacing of the pavements in Duke Street Hill and Tooley Street introduce to this bustling, but, nonetheless, architecturally staid environment, a Constructivist dynamic. Associations with Naum Gabo come to mind, but equally the geometrically incisive and materially dramatic intentions of the French revolutionary architects are recalled by this object. The adjacency of stone needle and glazed Tourist Centre, with all the differentiations in translucency that are technically available, allows each to stand on its own, as fragments towards a whole, reversible if need be, but finally creating a considered continuity in the public realm.

The borough of Southwark has been considerably altered since the reconstruction of Shakespeare's Globe Theatre with the new Tate Modern to its side. A new footbridge connecting north and south London on the axis of St Paul's Cathedral, as well as a new underground station for Southwark, part of the Jubilee Line has made a positive impact on the area known as Bankside. EPA's intervention, small and discreet as it appears, is part of the mosaic of improvements that in total have made a remarkable change for the better in the design of the public domain of the borough.

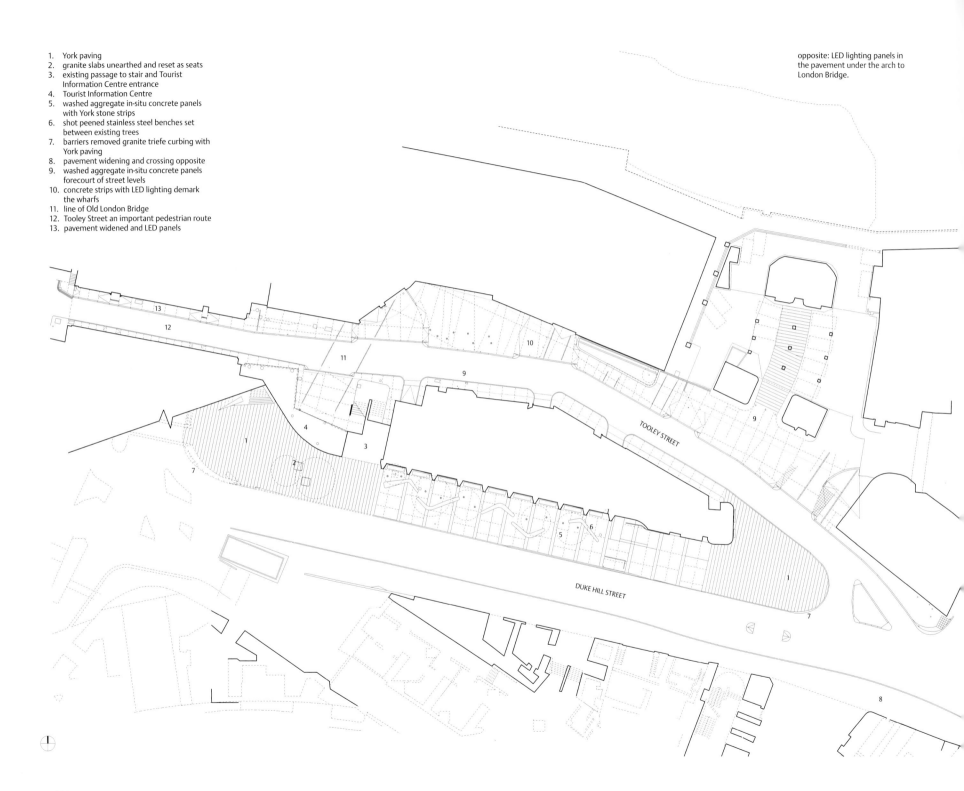

1. York paving
2. granite slabs unearthed and reset as seats
3. existing passage to stair and Tourist Information Centre entrance
4. Tourist Information Centre
5. washed aggregate in-situ concrete panels with York stone strips
6. shot peened stainless steel benches set between existing trees
7. barriers removed granite triefe curbing with York paving
8. pavement widening and crossing opposite
9. washed aggregate in-situ concrete panels forecourt of street levels
10. concrete strips with LED lighting demark the wharfs
11. line of Old London Bridge
12. Tooley Street an important pedestrian route
13. pavement widened and LED panels

opposite: LED lighting panels in the pavement under the arch to London Bridge.

TOOLEY STREET

DUKE HILL STREET

Benches and resurfacing to Duke
Hill Street.

Granta Park
South Cambridgeshire

With the experience of working for Stanhope Properties, Eric Parry Architects together with the landscape architects Latz and Partner, from Munich, have been able to secure a master planning scheme for a life sciences park on the rapidly developing periphery of Cambridge. As a magnet of bio-technological and scientific industries, Cambridge University has become the nucleus for newly founded companies in southern England.

1:10000

previous page: The south wing of the Amenity Building, which faces the county standard cricket pitch at the centre of the park. The storm water lake is to the centre and right of the photograph.

1. new roundabout on the Roman road (now passed by dual carriageway)
2. entrance avenue mature oak trees and security cabin
3. main access road, cycleway and pedestrian walkway to Granta Park
4. central meadow
5. county standard cricket pitch

6. storm water retention lake
7. building plots
8. green fingers—joining woodland to the central landscape
9. wind breaks planted between the larger building plots some of which are up to 120 m deep
10. parking groves for 2.000 cars

11. River Granta and surrounding woodland
12. The Welding Institute, series of industrial buildings loosely grouped around the eighteenth century Abington Hall
13. original avenue leading to the hall
14. the Abington villages

Part of the masterplan design and fly-through sequence.

Masterplan perspective.

Granta Park was identified as a possible development in the early 1990s in order to absorb the demand for green field sites for one of the most expansive industries at the turn of the century. Located near the Granta river, seven miles south of Cambridge, the site lies west of the Welding Institute (TWI), which will build a major research centre for itself in the new science park. The triangular plot of land was developed around a series of lowered terraces and a grey water pond, which form a focus and cultural nucleus: a cricket pitch and a club house (properly called Amenities Building, designed by Eric Parry Architects) establish a village atmosphere, around which the laboratories and offices gather.

In collaboration with Latz and Partner, EPA have been co-authors of a design guide for the construction of new landscape and buildings within the science park. Here, EPA have been able to express preferences, which have been implicit in other schemes. For instance, in ecological terms, passive rather than active (high-tech, intensive maintenance, expensive procurement) systems are to be preferred. The siting and configuration of each building should maximise the potential with respect to natural light and passive ventilation. Glazing should account for around 30 per cent of the external envelope, thus excluding so-called "high-tech" fully glazed double-skin solutions. Furthermore, a clear urban culture is to be realised by establishing principal facades towards the cricket pitch. Parking is to be accommodated in groves, and surface water systems between buildings should address grey water management. Most explicit in terms of the formation of character of the science park are the following statements and requirements: "The predominant character of Granta Park is determined by the landscape. A variety of building forms and sizes are expected on Granta Park. Buildings on Granta Park are placed between the natural woodland surrounding the site, reinforced by additional planting and parking groves, and the parkland heart. The intention is that buildings respond to the sylvan setting, are light in character, environmentally responsive with shadow-creating devices and a sense of shelter rather than fortress. Buildings should be a reflection of utility rather than style."

The landscape design by Peter and Anneliese Latz is based on an understanding of the history of the site. Located adjacent to a Roman road, the woodland envelops the rising of the river Granta and incorporates the remnants of the eighteenth and nineteenth century landscape around Abington Hall (now part of the TWI campus). There are also remnants of the military occupation in World War II, including landfill that followed the extraction of gravel, and the accumulation of toxic waste from farming over the last half century. Latz and Partner evolved a series of landscape principles, starting with a plan for water. With the landfill removed, the former tip was the obvious location for the storm water retention lake. Instead of piping rainwater away, the water was to follow rivulets through the landscape and all the building plots were designed and levelled to this goal. As a part of this strategy a grey and black water system with spiral reed beds was devised which may be adopted at a future date. Dams at strategic points on the

rivulets allow for extreme volumes of water without taking the lake levels beyond the limits of the stratigraphy of the planting regime, which is based on the (relatively low) seasonal rainfall in East Anglia. The central landscape focuses on the cricket pitch. At the initiation of the developer, this has replaced a pitch formerly on the landfill site—an unusual clause in the office leases requires each tenant to provide a cricket team. The rules of this quintessentially English game posed a challenge to the landscape designers but the levelled pitch is beautifully absorbed within a Bridgemanesque stepped section. The palette proceeds from the square through the outfield and self-sustaining meadow mix to the water-edge planting, which is slashed by the rivulets and their rough stone borders. It is a working landscape rather than a primarily formal response and resonates well with the purpose of the site. Then there are the patterns of movement. The roads are edged in granite setts that form water conduits and allow new entrances

to be made to building plots. They are lined on either side by an avenue of lime trees. On the inner (landscape) side, a generous pedestrian and cycle way is formed by a second row of trees of more varied species and surfaced in bound gravel. More than 2,000 cars are accommodated in 'parking groves'—heavily planted low-density zones that reinforce the perimeter woodland; when mature this will make an interesting set of spaces, with or without cars. To the north the natural woodland is connected to the new central landscape by 'green fingers' that contain lightly planted paths. To the south the larger plots are defined by wind breaks—a traditional agrarian idea that in time will visually shield the office 'farmyards' from one another and subdue the prevailing wind. The entrance is lined by semi-mature Hungarian oaks. Through constraints of time, money and craftsmanship, many of the landscape intentions were diluted yet a robust framework has been created, based on ecological aspirations.

1:50

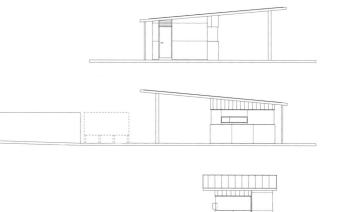

1:250

Street furniture and security cabin.

Granta Park from the air. The 35 hectares science park adjoins the existing TWI research facility at Abington Hall.

In contrast to Stockley Park, where the large landscape element is given over to an out-of-sight golf course (albeit with additional ponds between groups of office buildings), Granta Park has put its sole asset at the visual centre. All major and minor viewing axes are focused on the cricket pitch, the meadow and rivulets, and the combination of innovative technology and traditional rituals is a synthesis often sought by EPA. This underlying interest is expressed in the Amenities Building, containing the changing room facilities for the cricket grounds, a cafe as well as offices for the management of the park. The configuration with the splay recalls the office building for Stockley Park, and indeed, the different orientations of the long facades were the reasons for the building's composition: almost following the direction of the road on the northern side and facing the cricket pitch on the southern side, thereby also offering a closing gesture. Materially speaking, the two-storey club house consists of a concrete 'table' at ground floor and steel frame at first floor, an economical solution which provides fire protection. Here too, the external cladding of sheet metal panels (aluminium and titanium zinc) act in counterpoint to the rural appearance with the saddle roof. Its unusual geometry originates in the siting of the configuration, recalling also the experiments in the design of the roofs carried out for the Sussex Innovation Centre.

Combining the skills of the landscape designers and the architects results in an overall embedding of buildings within a basically formed dished enclosure, framed by mature woodland on the perimeter and accentuated by a peripheral expanse of water. In between these poles are delicately poised street lights, groves shrouding car parks and numerous edifices that appear like distant spectators of a test match. There is a bucolic calm at Granta Park, different to the pseudo-English picturesque garden of many business parks thanks to the deliberate placement of a geometrically ordered playing field at the centre of the development. This is the difference between the continuation of an unquestioned tradition and the conscious attempt to root the contemporary culture within a common heritage.

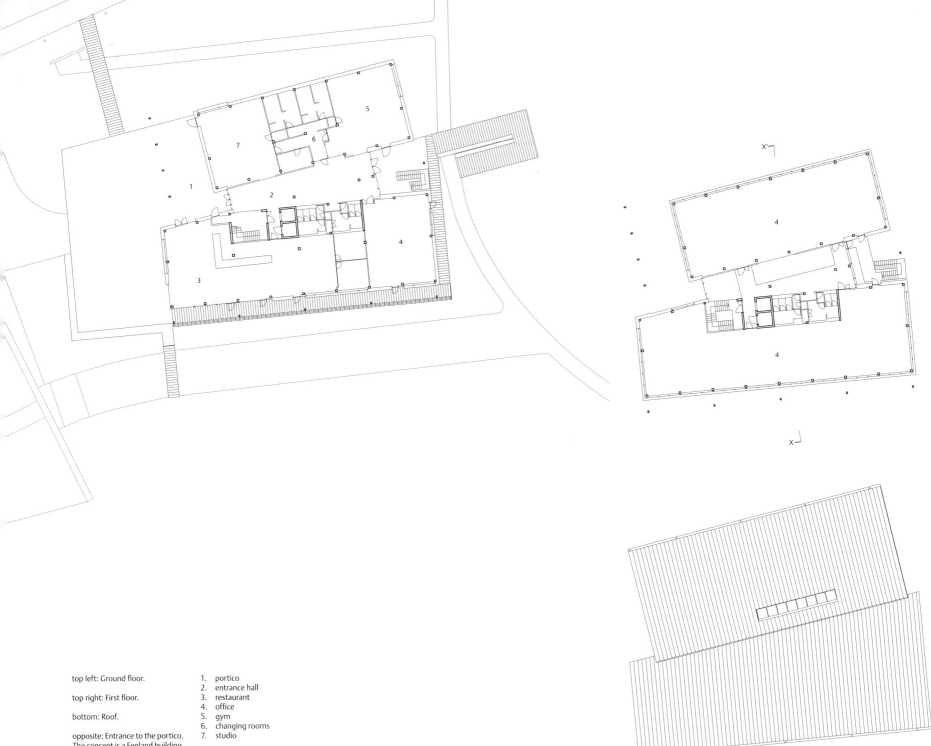

top left: Ground floor.

top right: First floor.

bottom: Roof.

opposite: Entrance to the portico.
The concept is a Fenland building,
raised off the surface of the ground.

1. portico
2. entrance hall
3. restaurant
4. office
5. gym
6. changing rooms
7. studio

1:500

1:250

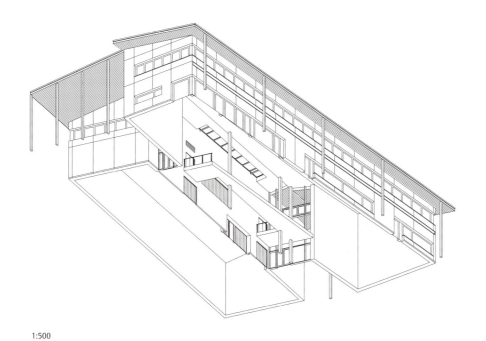

1:500

top left: Section X–X'.

bottom left: Isometric.

right: Model of the
Amenity Building.

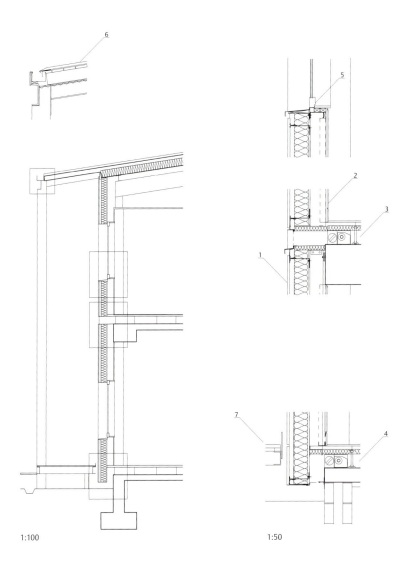

1:100

1:50

The wall is fabricated from pre-weathered titanium zinc panels, up to 4 m in height and 250 mm in width, fixed to horizontal rails and backed by 150 mm semi-rigid insulation and lined internally with two 12.5 mm layers of dense plasterboard. The horizontal joints reflect the floor heights, the window sill and head horizons and the slots on the south and north elevations. The slots allow air to be drawn into the first floor raised floor zone by means of tangential blowers, as part of the passive energy strategy for the building. Fresh air to the ground floor is drawn from beneath the skirt of the cladding. The windows, doors and sliding doors are fabricated from extruded aluminium sections and Pilkington Suncool glass. The roof finish is titanium zinc with standing seams on tanalised boarding and self-supporting liner trays.

1. titanium zinc wall panels
2. dense plasterboard panels
3. first floor fresh air inlet
4. ground floor fresh air inlet
5. aluminium windows
6. titanium zinc standing ream roof
7. boarded walkway and bench

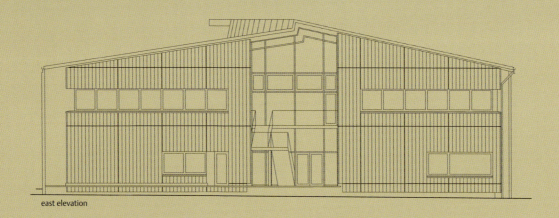

east elevation

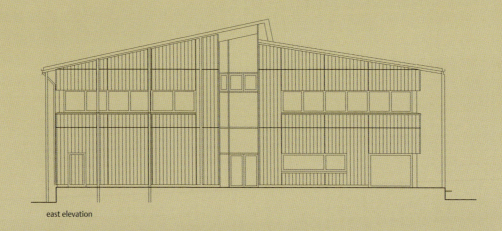

east elevation

154

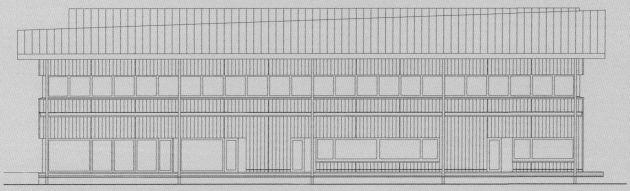

south elevation

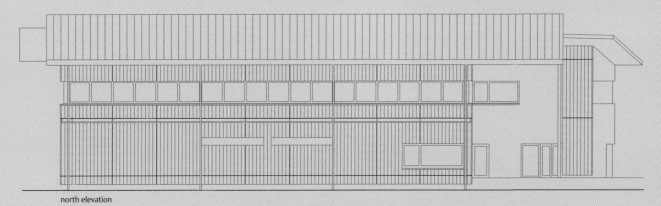

north elevation

1:250

Mandarin Oriental
Hotel Spa
London

In the course of London's firm establishment as a destination not only for the average tourists, but especially for the discerning traveller, a number of formerly glorious hotels of the late nineteenth century, much run down over the post-World War II years as a result of corporate expansion and resultant neglect in the actual running and maintenance of these "take-over" objects, were bought by international hotel chains as so-called flagships in various countries. In the late 1990s, the Hong Kong-based Mandarin Oriental Hotel Group purchased the Hyde Park Hotel, constructed in 1889 as a gentlemen's boarding house, which is strategically located to draw the views from Knightsbridge, Brompton Road and Sloane Avenue, and which in turn has commanding views across Hyde Park.

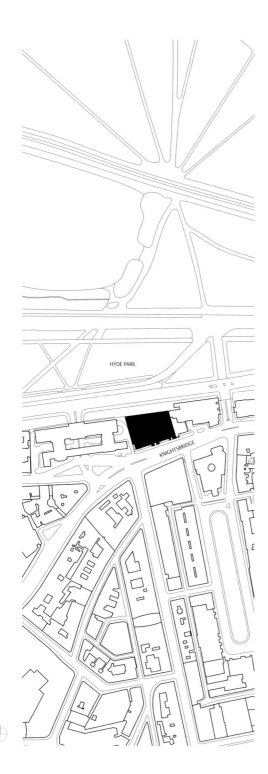

HYDE PARK

KNIGHTSBRIDGE

6

2   1   5

3

4

The hotel straddles the urban   1. reception rooms
density of Knightsbridge and the   2. ballroom
open vistas of the Park to the north. 3. upper level spa
                                       4. lower level spa
                                       5. Knightsbridge
                                       6. Hyde Park

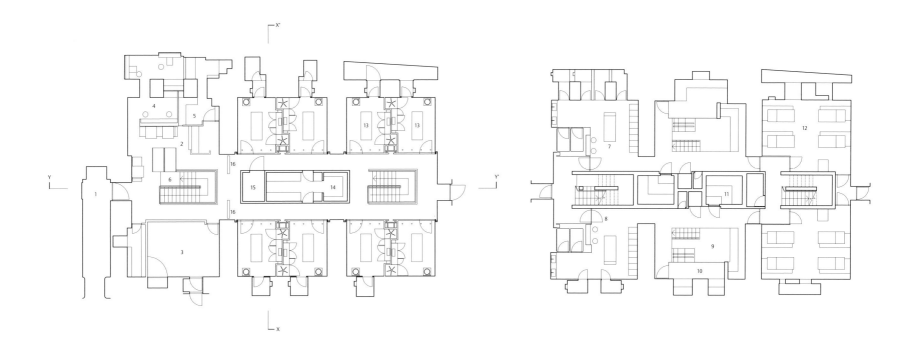

Along with the Royal Yacht Club and the French Embassy to its eastern side, and the Barracks of the Royal Horse Guards on its western side, the department stores Harrods (since the 1980s under the ownership of the Egyptian Al-Fayed brothers) and Harvey Nichols (also since the 80s under the ownership of the Hong Kong business man Dickson Poon) to the immediate south and Buckingham Palace not far, the now renamed Mandarin Oriental London is located in the most desirable location that the capital can offer.

The new owner invested extensively to create a luxury hotel equivalent to its Hong Kong headquarters. Aside from the refurbishment of all of the bedrooms, which in their original states accommodated bachelors

as part of the boarding facility, taking its clues from the Albany in Piccadilly and the clubs of Pall Mall, the reception and restaurant facilities were all redesigned to truly serve a hotel clientele. It now contains two hundred double bedrooms and suites, two restaurants, the by now common business centre, various banqueting rooms and the spa, designed by Eric Parry Architects. The expectations raised by the exterior of the late Victorian building with its red brick and stone institutional character was served in the detailing of the new upper ground floor spaces. Thus the reception counter, the dining spaces (Adam Tihany), corridors and bedrooms have been redeveloped in a restrained international hotel classicist manner. In a few years time most visitors and some architectural historians would not be able to detect the new from the original.

View toward reception from the treatment room corridor.

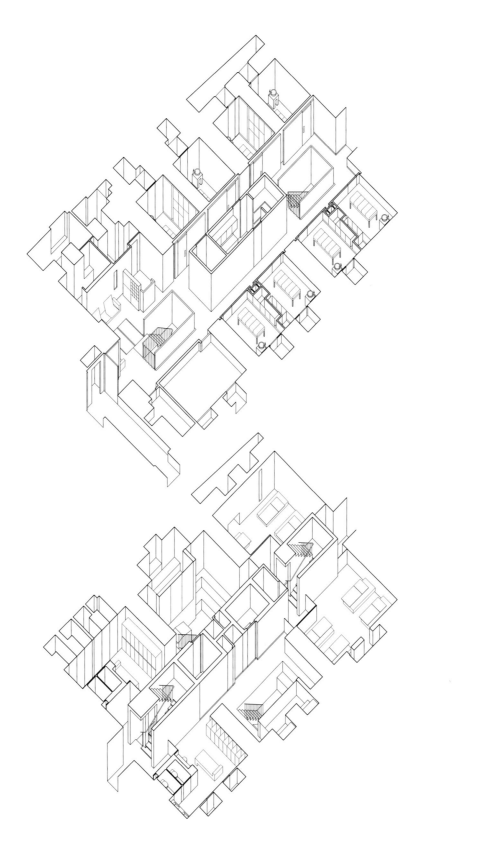

1:250

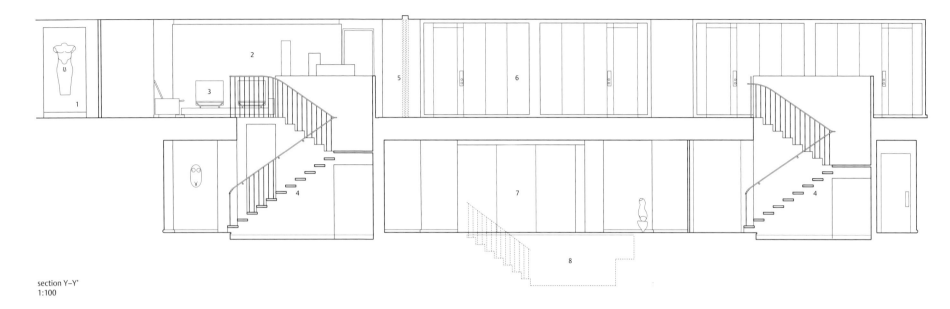

section Y–Y'
1:100

The difference in expression could not be greater than between this and the spa in the lower ground floor and basement in the northeastern corner of the block. Creating the transition between the world of heavily grained marble and mahogany, classically profiled skirtings, handrails and cornices, a world that is the appropriate response to the location of the hotel at the hub of the capital of a past empire, and that of contemporaneous introspective relaxation, physical exercise, quiet treatment and individual ritual has been achieved by taking advantage of both the overall underground approach as well as by specific axial and cross-axial articulations. Thus, descending by stairs from the upper ground level, a large glass-encased lobby is reached at the lower ground floor, which separates the spa and exercise facilities from the proposed but unbuilt Chinese restaurant. Alternatively, entering directly from the main vestibule at raised street level, a half flight of stairs takes the visitor directly to the corridor that connects the spa and the exercise rooms. At the end of the corridor, a highlit hermaphroditic torso hewn from Indian basalt is set against a large panel of dark grey semi-matte stone, bidding welcome. Colour composition and figure set the tone for the experience of the spa.

An arrival space with a reception desk, three wicker caned low seats across a pair of tatami mats set into the dark stained wooden floor, a picked

granite staircase leading to the lower floor, toplit fibrous curtains shrouding the view of the lateral corridors, all of these would normally be considered anything else but calm, in combination with the dominant continuous space beyond the fibrous curtains and the seemingly monolithic stair with its bronze handrails, it attains a calm centredness, which allows the visitor to properly prepare him or herself for the treatment. In addition to the architecture reinforcing an atmosphere of calm, the visitor is advised by the spa staff to arrive well before the treatment proper begins, in order to prepare oneself for the various spas and rituals. The spas, together with the sanarium, a milder version of a sauna, steam room, vitality pool with mineral water and hydrotherapy body jets and attendant rest rooms are located in the stone-lined basement. The visitor progresses through any one of these before re-emerging on the timber-lined lower ground floor for one of the ritual treatments. These have been developed from Chinese, Ayurvedic, European, Balinese, Oriental and Aman Indian traditions and are applied in one of the eight individual treatment rooms.

With the spa, EPA has been able to merge an idealised programme with an abstract poetic conception of architecture. The ritual of treatment offered at the spa is a congenial process that accompanies the architectural

1. sculpture placed over reflective water basin
2. lacquer wall
3. furniture Azumi/Hughes
4. granite slab stair over water basins
5. light curtain
6. horse hair panelled corridor to treatment rooms
7. glass-fronted steam rooms adjacent to treatment pool
8. treatment pool

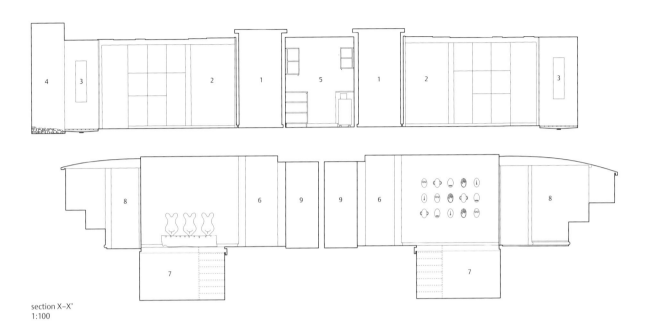

section X–X'
1:100

promenade. The visitor's pace is measured, circular in the use of the overall sequence as well as in the specific area of the spa. The division in the predominantly visible materials of stone and wood symbolise the worlds of the archaic and the refined, the visceral and the epidermic, the active and the passive.

The stone-lined pool with its various in-built seats and ledges, its lateral lighting and adjacent steam room, veiled only by a luminescent sheet of glass from the pool itself, is relatively small, as are all the spaces. The basement voids between park wall and hotel wall have been filled in such a way as to achieve a logical and yet not simply inevitable sequence of personalised as opposed to minute spaces. The almost diploid space of the vitality pool and steam room allows each of these areas to feel larger than they are. Similarly, the rest room and the treatment rooms take advantage of the former doorways and areas, in which gravel on the ground and indirect lighting now emanates to give a sense of an expanded quasi external space to the individual cell. Here the principle of borrowed space from Chinese and Japanese landscape architecture is used, as well as the techniques used by James Turrell for the creation of a sense of calm mystery through careful light design. The use of relatively large openings extending

the dimension of small spaces has been employed by numerous twentieth century architects including Adolf Loos. Loos' definition of the theatre box that overlooks a large space beyond, that is, the auditorium, is a helpful way to overcome the dimensional constraints of small cells. The design of the spa thus uses the irregular openings and former external spaces to fully establish an order of calm on the interior and filling the remaining spaces according to the diverse auxiliary programmes.

A similar sense of being part of two worlds at the same time is experienced on descending the stone stairs. The solid granite treads rise over a pebbled water basin, as if part of a river embankment, and their central vertical supports frame an opening that creates the sense of spatial extension. With its continuous lining in an upright direction, the stone enclosure acts like a telescope from the stone-lined basement rising to the lower ground floor, the lower floor thus announces itself by means of the two stair volumes. The bronze handrails balusters are alternatively offset within the plane of the stair's direction, so that no lateral stabiliser is required. In a way, this is a minimal solution in distinction to a visually simpler version, that, however, would be less effective in structural terms.

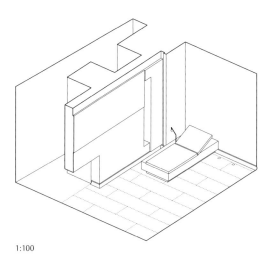

1:100

Relaxation room. Fibrous plaster wall relief with low level openings and dry garden beyond.

The Spa's ambience is determined by the extensive use of picked and hoved granite, generally giving the interior a cavernous character. Together with glass doors and room enclosures, reflective pools, ledges and cut backs, the Spa not so much pretends to a pre-historic environment as, for instance, Peter Zumthor's spa in Vaals does, but synthesises the massiveness and homogeneity of surface stone with the ingenuity of the subtle liveliness of sculpted busts and torsos.

The treatment rooms are similarly finely balanced cocoon-like spaces with microtextured surfaces, such as horse hair for the doors and outer partitions and on the three inner sides an off-white *craquelé* lacquer. These surfaces are expressed as layers, they pretend nothing else than being surface thick. In this way, the skirting and the cornice become recesses, while each treatment room is represented as a separate unit by the construction of flash gaps, themselves backlit with fluorescent lights. The doors to the treatment rooms thus appear as by-the-way instances along the length of horse hair covered wall panels. On the one hand, then, each room is announced to the outside, yet on the other, the door is discreetly merged with the fabric covering, a seeming paradox that is typical of the attitudes sought by the clients of this spa. On the ceiling of each room is a plaster relief inspired by Ben Nicholson's

constructivist *White Relief* of 1935. The entire space, complete with its borrowed miniature garden, speaks of care, refinement and discreet luxury.

Post-enlightenment architectural principles from Semper to Gray come together in a seemingly understated way. Experience at first hand show the richness and diversity of each corner, each junction, each space. The Spa's user is truly pampered in accordance with the exclusive charges that are raised. EPA has demonstrated with the Spa that difficult historical contexts do not have to be answered in an inconsiderate normative way, on the contrary, that it is entirely within keeping to respond with clearly articulated compositions and materials in order to achieve a visual density and personal experience that not only meets the expectations of a widely travelled user, but that it can be exceeded.

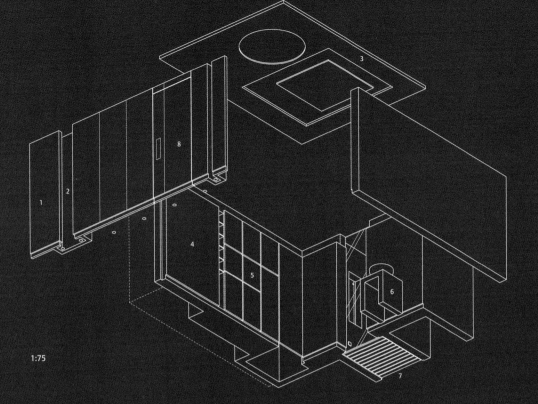

treatment room worm's eye axonometric

1. horse hair wall panel
2. light slot between rooms
3. fibrous plaster relief ceiling
4. lacquer panel
5. storage cabinets
6. Azumi basin stand
7. shower
8. flush door

1:75

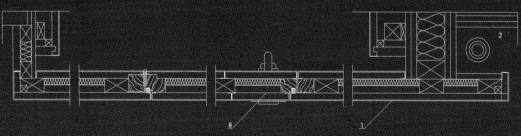

1:10

section
1:10

1. horse hair wall panel and flush door
2. corridor
3. treatment room
4. push plate

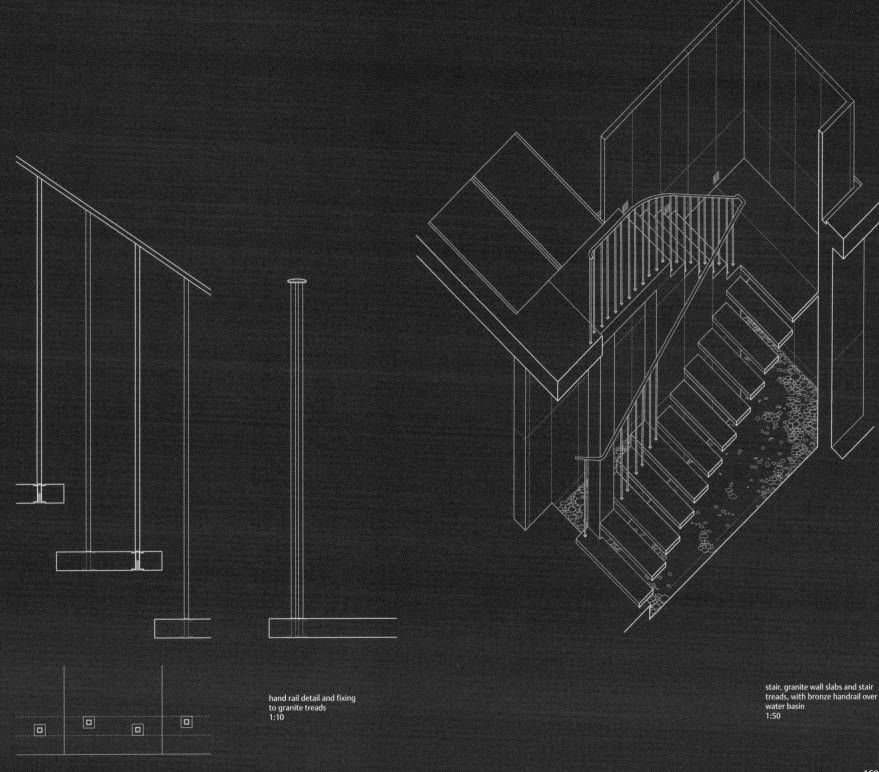

hand rail detail and fixing
to granite treads
1:10

stair, granite wall slabs and stair
treads, with bronze handrail over
water basin
1:50

169

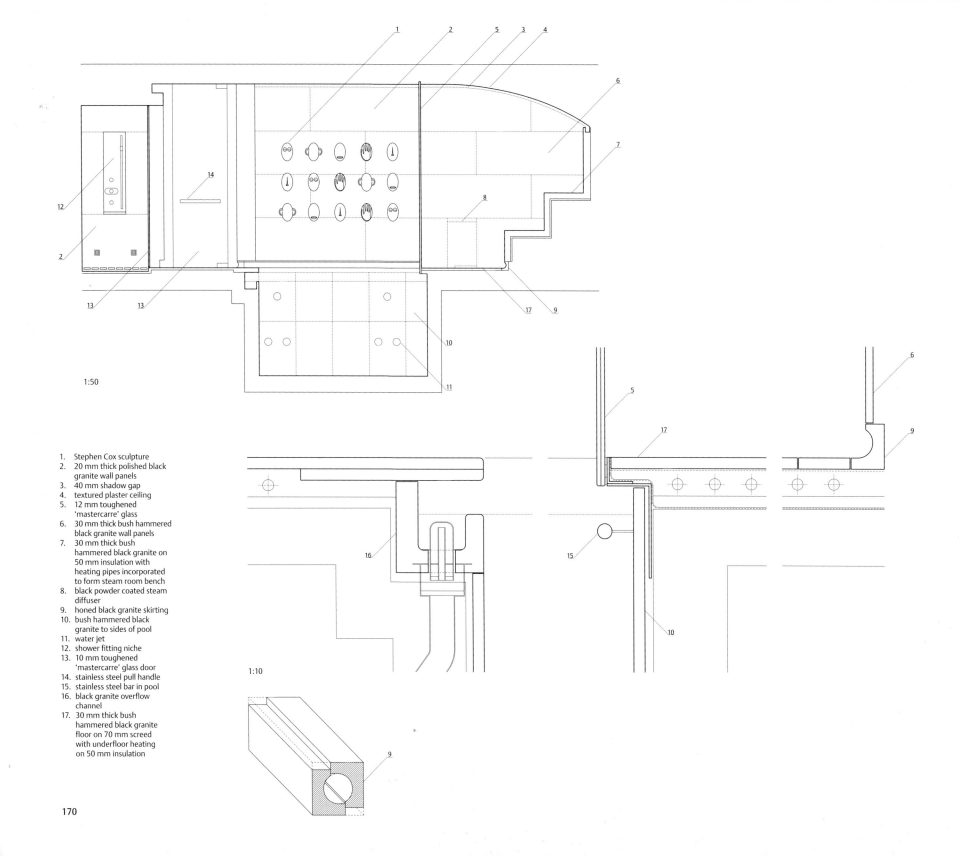

1:50

1. Stephen Cox sculpture
2. 20 mm thick polished black granite wall panels
3. 40 mm shadow gap
4. textured plaster ceiling
5. 12 mm toughened 'mastercarre' glass
6. 30 mm thick bush hammered black granite wall panels
7. 30 mm thick bush hammered black granite on 50 mm insulation with heating pipes incorporated to form steam room bench
8. black powder coated steam diffuser
9. honed black granite skirting
10. bush hammered black granite to sides of pool
11. water jet
12. shower fitting niche
13. 10 mm toughened 'mastercarre' glass door
14. stainless steel pull handle
15. stainless steel bar in pool
16. black granite overflow channel
17. 30 mm thick bush hammered black granite floor on 70 mm screed with underfloor heating on 50 mm insulation

1:10

170

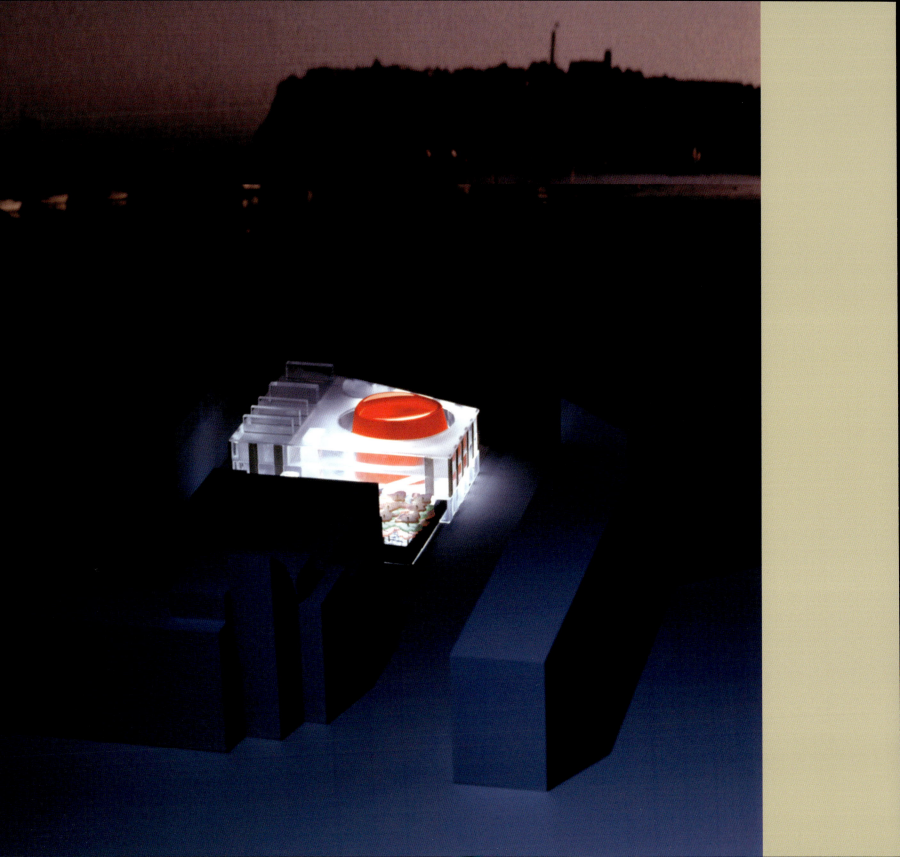

Welsh Assembly
Cardiff

The shortlisted competition submission for the Welsh Assembly building situated in the disused docklands area of Cardiff Bay was the opportunity to design a major public building. That it was not built is a reflection of the hegemony of architectural politics in the UK.

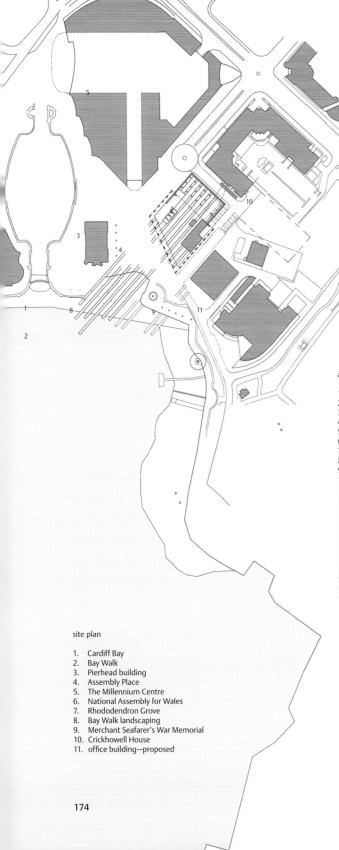

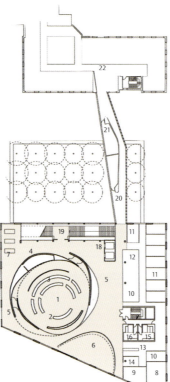

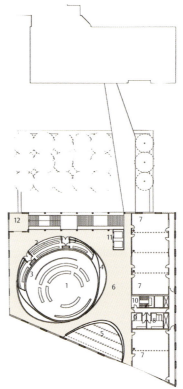

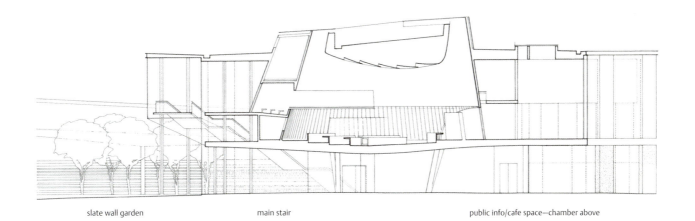

slate wall garden   main stair   public info/cafe space—chamber above

Assembly room sectional model.

Views to Cardiff Bay.

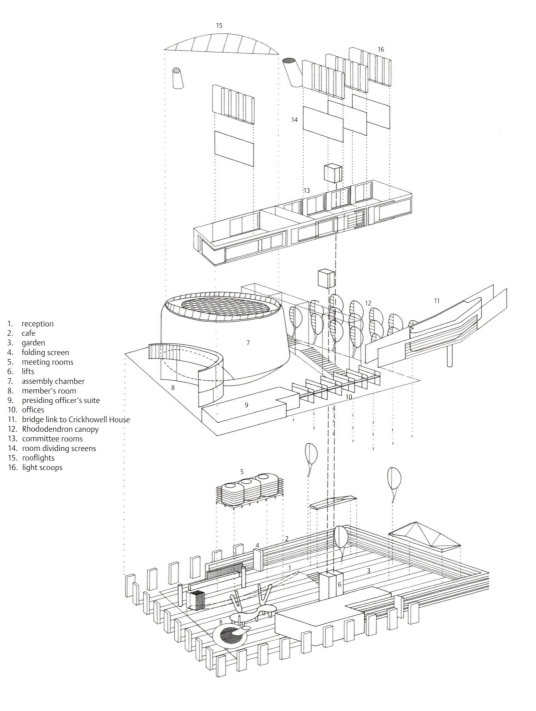

1. reception
2. cafe
3. garden
4. folding screen
5. meeting rooms
6. lifts
7. assembly chamber
8. member's room
9. presiding officer's suite
10. offices
11. bridge link to Crickhowell House
12. Rhododendron canopy
13. committee rooms
14. room dividing screens
15. rooflights
16. light scoops

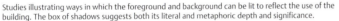
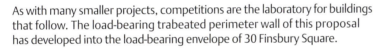

Studies illustrating ways in which the foreground and background can be lit to reflect the use of the building. The box of shadows suggests both its literal and metaphoric depth and significance.

As with many smaller projects, competitions are the laboratory for buildings that follow. The load-bearing trabeated perimeter wall of this proposal has developed into the load-bearing envelope of 30 Finsbury Square.

The metaphor for this project was the House of Conversation. The Assembly Building will be a long overdue national meeting place in which discussion should be encouraged to develop in as many ways as possible. Our proposal aims to nurture dialogue by providing appropriate architectural settings that range from; the informal—in the cafe, on the pavement, in the garden: the semi-formal—the ground level meeting rooms, the exhibition spaces, the public gallery; the formal—Committee rooms, the Assembly Chamber.

Cities that have a close relationship with the sea like Venice and Amsterdam share the excitement of mercantile adventure and distant relationships—Cardiff Bay is rekindling this potential and already citizens are rediscovering the waterfront. From this successful public space will evolve.

We imagine the urban space in front of the building will be a place for the expression of national celebration and on occasion grief. Whilst our proposal provides a defining edge it also encourages entrance. Unlike most other parliament buildings the ground is seen as an extension of the public space—like the covered stoa of the ancient city or the open undercroft of many market town council chambers our space offers catalysts for casual or arranged encounters.

The cyber cafe, enclosed garden and covered space with information points to access events internationally, nationally and locally all contribute to the public life of the ground floor. This space aims to promote an atmosphere of creative enquiry and observation—perhaps not unlike the tradition of the eighteenth century coffee house in which pamphlets and political initiatives were routinely formulated. It should be notable for its social inclusiveness and accessibility. To stress its groundedness the material of the ground floor will be a combination of Welsh slate and granite. To the north it will become a garden of moss and fern covered slate slabs out of which the rhododendron and birch trees will grow. The same surface extends out to a bay where it fragments and is absorbed by the water. The metamorphosis from chaos and nature to artifice is evident in the passage from open water to sheltered garden.

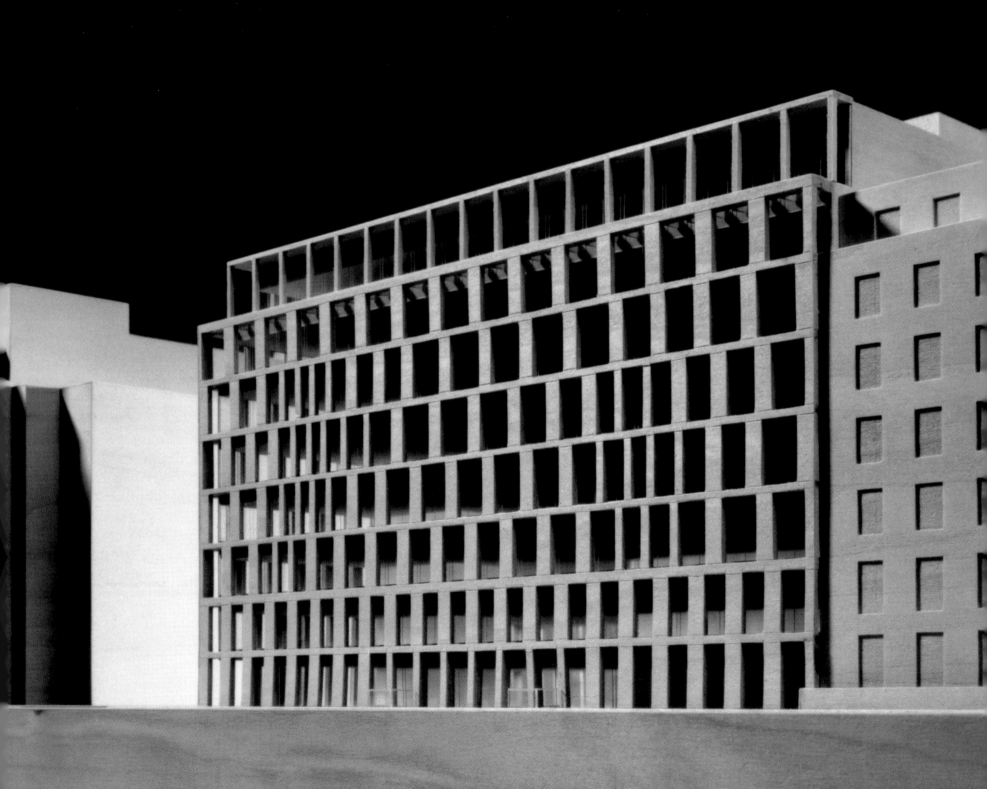

30 Finsbury Square
London

The most ambitious design by Eric Parry Architects to date is an office building in the London Borough of Islington, a relatively poor inner city district neighbouring the richest: the City of London, its financial district.

1799

1879

1929

1999

1:1500

previous page: 1:200 timber model of the building submitted for planning approval, view from Finsbury Square.

left: Historical development.

1799 originally laid out by George Dance in 1777. By the end of the century the square is faced by 60 terraced houses.

1879 the density has increased and some properties have been amalgamated.

1929 commercial properties begin to dominate but the original west terrace remains intact.

1999 the Square is shared by less than ten commercial occupiers. No 27–30 shown hatched.

top right: View of the square as existing from the southwest.

bottom right: Plan of the Square showing proposals by Latz and Partner. We undertook a use pattern study of the existing Square. The building proposal which in urban terms required the design of the enclosing wall to the Square is also in dialogue with the Latz proposal which involved the removal of the petrol stations and single level basement car park and included an acoustic glass screen to the west side of the Square, the creation of a sunken garden with the popular bowling green repositioned at the centre; to the east a steel framed pavilion structure, reusing elements of the demolished facade rehouses the existing restaurant with kiosks for other amenities. The roof to this structure incorporates photovoltaics to power water movement in the new groves of trees to either side of the green. Echoing the heaviest pedestrian movement across the Square. An avenue of trees is proposed to the east side. Because of the contentious nature of the development this brilliant scheme has sadly foundered on the rock of local politics.

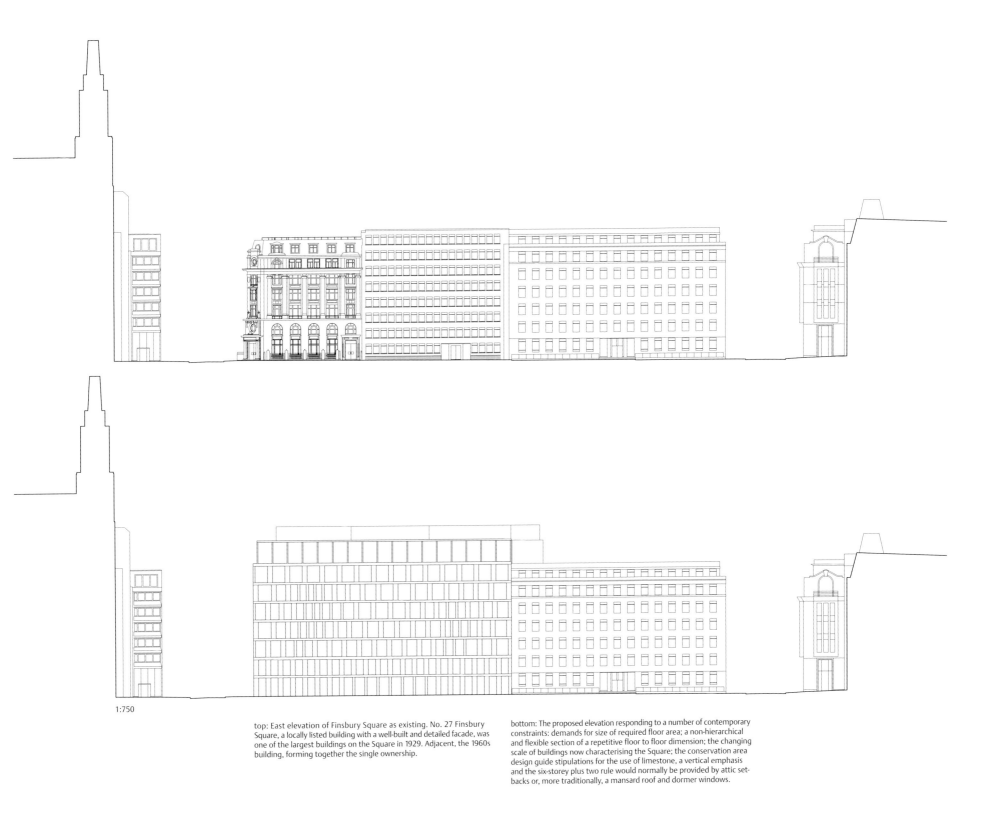

1:750

top: East elevation of Finsbury Square as existing. No. 27 Finsbury Square, a locally listed building with a well-built and detailed facade, was one of the largest buildings on the Square in 1929. Adjacent, the 1960s building, forming together the single ownership.

bottom: The proposed elevation responding to a number of contemporary constraints: demands for size of required floor area; a non-hierarchical and flexible section of a repetitive floor to floor dimension; the changing scale of buildings now characterising the Square; the conservation area design guide stipulations for the use of limestone, a vertical emphasis and the six-storey plus two rule would normally be provided by attic set-backs or, more traditionally, a mansard roof and dormer windows.

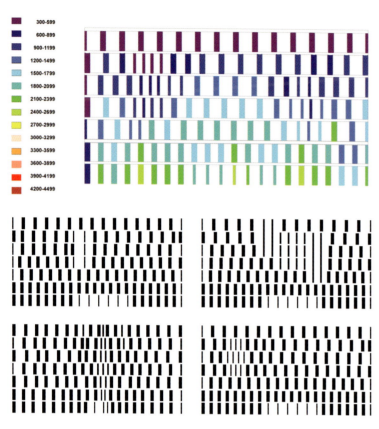

The City's unspoken characteristics are personal networks, a virtually non-existent public (some four and half thousand residential voters), tax-exempt guilds as one of the major landowners of key properties whose board members are recruited from the local businesses, church wardens whose members are also recruited from the local businesses, a local government—the Corporation of the City of London—that is barely answerable to Central government, a Lord Mayorship that is granted on the basis of "buggin's turn" (once a person is elected as an alderman, he or she joins a queue to "inherit" the title) and a territorial freedom that includes the power to force the reigning monarch to ask for the Corporation's permission in order to enter the City. Islington on the other hand had a reputation for being run by the "loony left" until one of its most prominent residents, Tony Blair, became Prime Minister. Benefiting from this neighbourhood, Islington is gradually experiencing an expanding office development on its southern edge.

The site of the office building for the pension fund of Scottish Widows on Finsbury Square is literally just a few yards outside the boundary of the City of London. As more of the City of London itself becomes developed with new office buildings (except for the churches and other monuments, nearly three quarters of the entire of the built fabric of the City has been constructed anew since World War II, the rest has been renovated on the interior), the number and size of potential development sites has

decreased such that investors have searched for suitable land beyond the curtilage of the City of London.

While the vast proportion of the financial district's fabric has been renovated or built anew over the last decades, conservationists have fought a rear-guard battle against extensive architectural and urban alterations. The most drastic change to the entire inner city, whether located in the City or in the adjoining boroughs, has been the shift in residential population: before World War II nearly a quarter of a million lived in this part of London, now only a few thousand do. The built substance therefore has been subject to this fundamental shift: residential units—Georgian terraced houses, Victorian tenements—have been demolished to make way for ever more sophisticated office buildings. The attendant affect on open space has been to use these for underground car parks wherever possible, a solution adopted for Finsbury Square. Its conversion to a treeless lawn was a consequence of World War II: an anti-aircraft gun emplacement had already removed the oval arrangement of vegetation so that the development of an underground car park complete with two petrol stations contributed to the space's barren appearance today. In their proposal for the office building on this square therefore, EPA asked Latz and Partner to present a new hard and soft landscaped environment to restore to the space a sense of unity in the tradition of London squares,

top left: Colour study showing weight distribution through piers.

bottom left: Four stages in the development of the elevation to Finsbury Square. Accumulative loads through eight floors and the length of facade with its responsiveness to the scale of the Square were important aspects of the composition.

right: 1:50 scale wood model of the corner of Christopher Street and Finsbury Square. At Square level the traditional area in front of the building is replaced by large glass pavement lights between piers that allow light in to the lower ground floor as does the set-back to the ground floor. The first floor is propped, and so the greatest accumulation of load is at the second floor and this is reflected in the larger depth of the precast horizontal edge beam at this level. Piers at second and first floor are aligned to create a rhythmic reflection to the inflection of those at the entrance to the building. The attic levels step back at sixth floor which creates a balcony open to the sky and, at seventh floor, a verandah enclosed by stainless steel stanchions and canopy. The tyranny of the office planning grid is disrupted by the rhythm of its stone piers. The stainless steel mullions reflect light outwards to the office face of the stone.

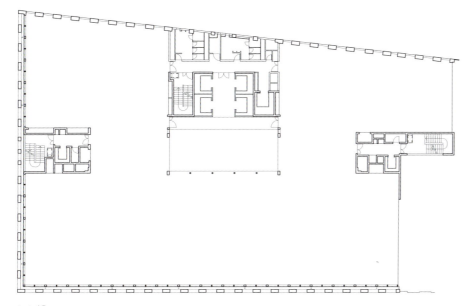

typical floor

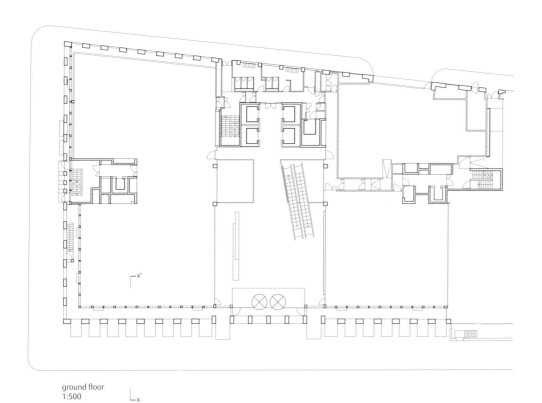

ground floor
1:500

x'

x

1:500 scale model of the Square (without the Latz and Partner landscape proposal for the Square).

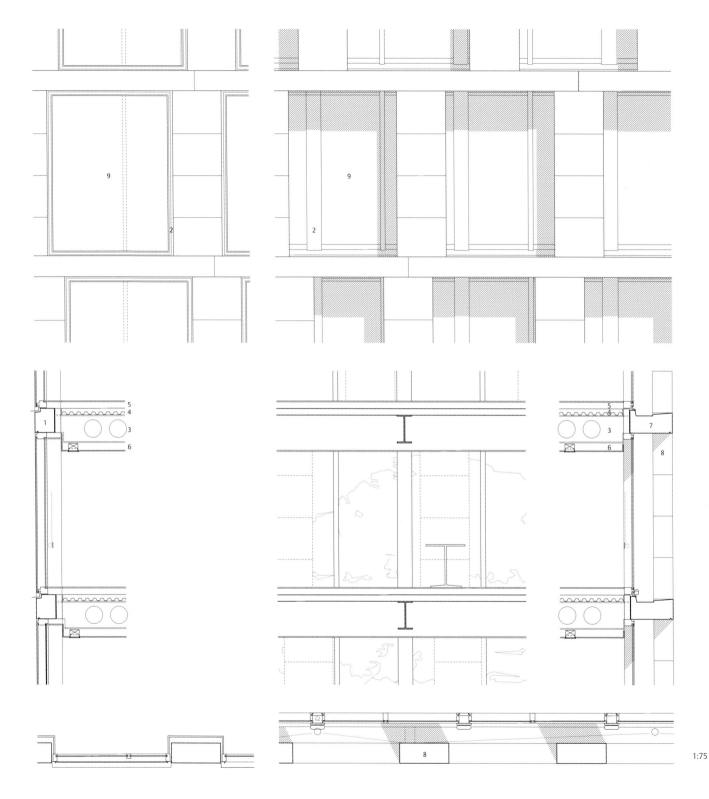

top left: Typical part elevation to Wilson Street. The glass plane is flush with the outer face of the stone piers. Because of the conflation of the two grids the mullions occur at varying points in the openings between piers.

top right: Typical part elevation to Finsbury Square. The horizontal precast concrete lintels pick up the load from cell beams spanning 15 m at 3 m centres. Solid stone piers support the lintels. Each pier is made of four blocks of stone 1000 x 400 mm on bed (but not exclusively). Each pier sits on a stooled horizontal bedding plane. Half a metre behind the stone is the glazing line. The 1.5 m office planning grid alternates between a thinner and thicker stainless steel capping, the latter to house rainwater pipes.

bottom left: Typical section through the wall, Wilson Street.
1. precast lintel
2. stainless steel framed glazing
3. cell beam
4. concrete deck
5. raised floor
6. ceiling and lighting zone

bottom right: Typical section through the wall.
7. precast lintel housing steel universal beam
8. stone pier, prefabricated and transported to site as a single unit
9. glazing

1:75

1:200 scale model.

to provide an amenity suggestive of rest and calm (a bowling green) amidst the bustle of the district and to screen, at least visually, if not acoustically, the heavy traffic along the opposite side of the office building designed by EPA. Regrettably, the Latz and Partner design has not been approved to date and looks as if it will stay on paper.

While London remains an international centre of financial exchange, taking advantage of its equivocal political and cultural attitude towards continental European integration (delayed membership of the common currency system) as well as its time difference, this process of tertiary industrialisation will continue. Computerisation has rationalised employment patterns in the tertiary industries, however, there appears to be an unsatiated demand for new office space. Vacancy rates of commercial property has been relatively low at the turn of the century and rents have been amongst the highest compared to international locations. All of this has contributed towards the continued construction of office buildings and, interestingly for architects, a discourse has developed over the remaining aspects still open to true design considerations.

A certain maturation in the definition of the work space has taken place for offices. Standard demands by clients of offices, whether developers for speculative buildings or owner occupiers, are to provide flexible, subdividable floor units, that can be reached from a set of common vertical circulation elements. Daylighting is not so much an issue given the extensive use of computer screens, that require glare-free and constant level lighting. For the upper market tertiary industry, all spaces must be air-conditioned, or capable of being air-conditioned (contrary to some continental European countries, in which regulations exist prohibiting additional energy demand for cooling and artificial ventilation). Demands for low initial costs, short construction periods, and light construction are also common. Prefabrication, steel sub-frames, sheet metal and glass with minimal in-situ concrete work are thus common. Glazing bars must be arranged at certain centres so as to allow for the subdivision of offices on the perimeter. The latter has implied a relatively tight range of grid dimensions acceptable to the office industry. At the same time, developers are keen to have a building that is visually unusual, indeed striking in order to increase the marketability of their product. Within these narrow bands of demands, some of which run counter to others, contemporary architects are searching ways by which they are able to satisfy their clients while entering the architects' own discourse on that which remains: the expression of values through architecture of the respective interpretation of a society's culture.

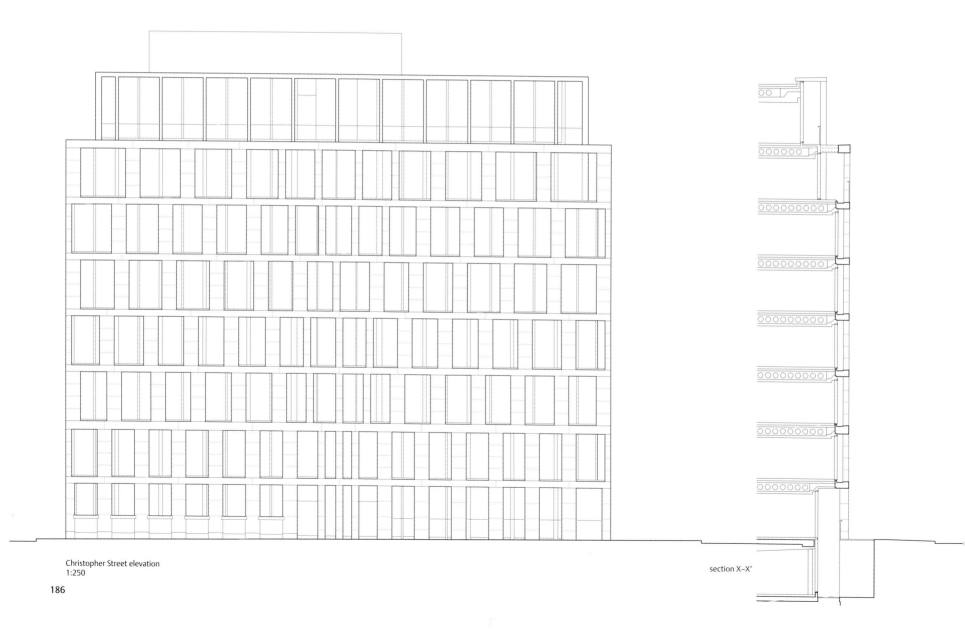

Christopher Street elevation
1:250

section X–X'

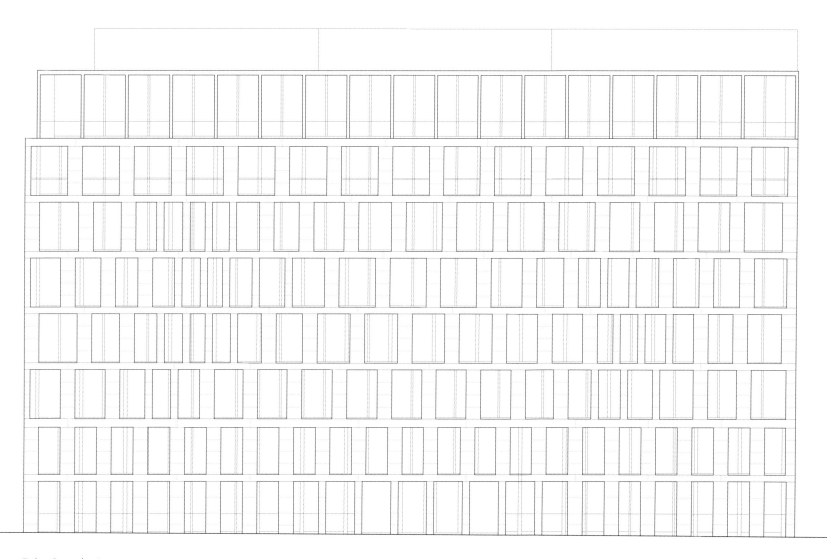

Finsbury Square elevation

The City of London is thus also the reference point for much advanced and ambitious office design. Some of the most spectacular edifices in this category have been designed by the offices of Arup Associates, Skidmore Owings and Merrill, Norman Foster, Richard Rogers and Michael Hopkins, to name a few. In these buildings, much is made of the modernist notion of rational repetition, the integration of the latest advances in technology, the expression of precision and smooth detailing. Regularity through exposed structure, systematisation through identical details for visible elements such as windows, corporate culture through discreet elegance are the hallmarks of these office buildings. Any such order achieved on the exterior is relatively independent of the flexible interior. Here partition, raised floor and false ceiling systems—more often than not installed by the tenant—are chosen on the basis of the lowest cost, have a short life-expectancy and are frequently unattractive. EPA's design for Finsbury Square is not likely to be privileged with a better fate. Its difference to the other schemes rests in the apparent disorder, or picturesqueness, of the facade in the distribution of the self-load-bearing masonry. Contrary to the otherwise extensive use of glass, metallic infill panels and polished granite cladding, EPA have chosen to provide a screen of limestone to establish a link with the surrounding stone-clad buildings. This layer of limestone formally provides two kinds of depth, where thinness normally rules—first, in terms of the thickness of each limestone pier itself and, secondly, in terms of the space between the piers and the glazing. In environmental terms, the limestone layer provides some shading to the fully glazed secondary layer behind the stonework.

In separating the representative 'skin' from the functional surface, EPA have given themselves a domain of autonomy that reclaims an urban role for architecture. The design satisfies the needs for office sub-division, as these walls—wherever they fall, with whichever regularity or irregularity—will now actually play in concert with the picturesque limestone screen.

Given the seeming irregularity of the stone screen, the office block as a whole appears less of a homogeneous mass than some of its neighbours, whether with a monotonous fenestration as those buildings of the 1950s or whether with neoclassical accents such as lateral wings and central porticos. Thus the transformation of the city into autistic blocks of tertiary industries is ameliorated at this instance, without breaking the formal link to its masonry neighbours.

The limestone pier pattern itself follows general structural rules of expressing reduced loading towards the top with echoes of circulation cores behind and judiciously placed 'disturbances' that create shifting visual centres and balances. An acknowledged precedent for EPA was the Town Hall Extension by Rafael Moneo for Murcia, 1998, in which the open loggias and the irregular composition of stone pillars towards the top of the town hall's principal facade create a degree of articulation that gives the narrow fronted building an appropriate weight to stand in context with the Baroque cathedral opposite. Prior to this, Alejandro de la Sota's Tarragona Offices of the Central Government, 1957, used the 'rupture' in the monumental masonry principal facade as a vehicle to criticise the powers that were—the offices were not to be affirmatively rationalist but expressively oppositional. In Peter Märkli's apartment block in Sargans, 1985, the four-storey reinforced concrete street facade consists of a base with three layers of loggias screened by a regular grid of pillars that is broken in only a few fields to give an overall sense of disorder. This facade may evoke images of Le Corbusier's La Tourette, however, the conceptions are distinct, if not to say worlds apart. Märkli is interested in the distinction achieved by the intervention of difference—and not disorder—in the expression of a classically conceived architecture, Le Corbusier and Yannis Xenakis were interested in the notion of the aleatory within a confined dimension as a means of achieving a visually stimulating surface. EPA's approach is a synthesis of these approaches.

Archaic, colossal, representative yet dynamic, that is the visual effect of the self-load-bearing limestone piers for the Finsbury Square office building.

Märkli's apartment block consists of an in-situ reinforced concrete structure with the depth of the loggia as a relatively separate volume. It is, so to speak, a three-dimensional skin in front of the thermally insulated units. La Tourette and subsequent buildings with such formal concerns as Northwick Park Hospital have continuous floor plates with in-fill structural mullions. The corporate alternative to this is probably best exemplified by Gordon Bunshaft's Banque Lambert headquarters in Brussels, 1965, that is one of the last ideal types to defiantly uphold the principle of monolithic structural frame, albeit restricted to each floor construction. Cold bridges were no concern in those days. Since the first oil crisis in the early 1970s, all of this structural heroics has been rendered impossible by new building codes in most temperate climate zones. Architects had to think again. The acknowledgement of the separate layers took some time to take root. One of the logical conclusions was the consistent wrapping of structure by a cladding system. This, however, prevented the expression of structure, bringing about a sense of loss and frustration that in part could be argued to have led to sentiments favouring classical and, in its train, postmodern forms. The office building on Finsbury Square is a lateral entry into this discourse by adopting a number of unconventional, yet thoroughly well-known detailed design principles.

For instance, the use of transfer beams of reconstituted stone—they are pre-cast units that are 'whiter' using a dolomitic limestone aggregate but conceived as compatible, giving a quiet horizontal emphasis that reflects the sectional characteristics of the building—i.e. repetitive heights. It is a favourite theme in subsequent Western designs as for instance for bookcases as designed by Charlotte Perriand (presented in Tokyo in 1955). These transfer beams are structurally connected by shear plates to the steel cell beams at three m centres. The double layer does not, alas exist—it was intentional that the facade to Wilson Street (which is a typical street width) should be flush to register the distinction between it and the facade to Finsbury Square (which relates directly to Christopher Street). The junctions between each masonry element and between the piers and transfer beams speaks of the experience gained over the years by EPA, initially and continually via their exposure to the stone masons at the Château de Paulin, who are the cathedral restoration masons at Albi. The pleasure of stonework in conjunction with the precision that is possible relativises the high-tech arguments for certain materials more normatively associated with innovative technologies, more often than not merely ideologised science fiction: prefabrication and off-site manufacture are possible in any material, whether concrete, clay, plaster, steel, aluminium, glass, marble or limestone. EPA are demonstrating here that indeed anything is possible given ancient and modern technologies and that it is the cultural ambition that determines relevance, significance, coherence and the success of a realised concept.

No doubt any conscious architect with a critical mind is aware of the threats posed by a continuing division of labour. In the construction industry there is a noticeable increase in the number and type of specialists with an inversely proportionate decrease in responsibilities and shared knowledge. EPA's office design at Finsbury expresses this separation of different layers as documents of different constructional technologies and different responsibilities nevertheless brought together under the overall auspices, that is to say, the overall responsibility of the architects. The seeming disorder is thus fundamentally based on a broad understanding of the order of things. The Finsbury Square office building expresses the Roman principle of *dirigere*—divide and rule—as one option in the pursuit of clear architectural goals.

Projects Summary

Animation
Graphic Design Studios
London

The refurbishment of an existing building on a deep plot behind a terracotta facade. Once the Soho Club but more recently used by Capital Radio as a broadcasting school with triple-glazed sound booth windows on the street. Apart from upper floor offices and studios the challenge was to open up the facade to create a waiting area and reception and to connect this space via a passage to a double-height atrium and beyond that to the theatre of the animator's studio. The spatial mediation between street and deep interiority was influenced by the literature of nineteenth century Symbolism and a concurrent analysis of the work of Victor Horta.

C: Animation City & QDM
M&E: Max Fordham and Partner
SE: Michael Pereira
A: EP, MM, NG, CW
Date: 1986

Artists' Studios
London

The two artists lived in the same road in Camberwell but could not have differed more in the character and process of their work. Antony Gormley had just suffered the loss of a significant body of work in the storms of 1987 when the wall to his existing studio had collapsed. He required as large and as scaleless a space as possible, with a number of supporting rooms. The beginnings of his works *Field* and *Tree* (a figure carved from a storm felled tree), tested the limits of his new space. Tom Phillips needed an exhibition space, spaces for his Talfourd Press and a studio which are all relatively intimately scaled. Tom, who suffered from vertigo

found models the best tool rather than site visits for dialogue. When the first floor studio was complete but empty he made his first visit and told me not to worry he would soon "fuck it up"—by which he meant to breathe life into it.

C: Antony Gormley and Tom Phillips
PM: EPA
SE: Michael Pereira
A: EP, NG, WM
Dates: 1986–1988

Château de Paulin
Tarn, France

The current owner purchased the château in 1987 for the equivalent cost of a London town house–but with a large maintenance bill. There have been ten, or so, successive projects of different scale and type in five phases.

Phase 1—Conservation of the walls and renovation of the roofs; new machine and tool store with workshop. Phase 2—The tower; new entrance and wine cellar; kitchen and bridge. Phase 3—The chapel (first scheme) and dining table (first scheme). Phase 4—Swimming pool; courtyard paving and dining table. Phase 5—The chapel.

The château is formidably positioned and bears the brunt of extreme weather. On my first visit I watched clouds drift through my room and during the recent storms the wind was recorded at a constant 190 km per hour. The most recent project had to be redesigned to accommodate a likely collapse of supporting rock in the next one hundred years and in geological time the rest of the buildings are destined to follow.

C: Château de Paulin
M&E: Michael Popper Associates
SE: Dewhurst McFarlanes & Partners
A:
Phase 1 – EP, CW, PM, GH, WM
Phase 2 – EP, CW, PM, GH
Phase 3 – EP, CW, WM
Phase 4 – EP, RK
Phase 5 – EP, GEM, NM
Dates: 1987–ongoing

Pembroke College
Cambridge
Masterplan

As a result of a competitive interview in 1987 we were commissioned to make a study to determine where, on its site in central Cambridge, the college could put 100 new student rooms, a lecture/performance space and additional seminar and common rooms. The site has been in continuous and evolving occupation for 650 years. The outcome was a portfolio of drawings that included reconstructed plans of the college topography at four key historical periods, four alternative schemes for accommodation buildings and an outline scheme for the theatre. The favoured option was illustrated by a model. The drawings and proposals were explained in

a report with an accompanying analysis. The cultural mapping of a very rich history raised difficult questions including for instance the need to demolish a sound and well-built Master's Lodge. Given the complex internal politics of college life a well argued strategy was needed for the society to accept the largest building project in its history.

C: Master, Fellows and Scholars of Pembroke College, Cambridge
A: EP, PM, NG, WM, GH, CW
Date: 1988

Offices for Stanhope
London

This was our first brush with the world of commercial development—Stanhope were at the time building the massive Broadgate project. The commission resulted from a competition and being noticed at the *Four London Architects* exhibition at the 9H Gallery. An office fit out tests skills of ordering akin to urban design and detail akin to product design. This 2000 m² floor was completed in fifteen weeks from the beginning of design to client occupation. A generous reception space led to meeting rooms and beyond to a layout of cellular offices at the perimeter of the envelope. Now demolished.

C: Stanhope Properties plc
PM: Schal International
M&E: How Engineering Services Furniture
Consultants: Business Design Group
A: EP, NG, CW, MM, PM, KS, GH, MP, WM
Date: 1988

Ferry House
South Cambridgeshire

A design for a house on the site of a disused ferry crossing and tea house next to the river Cam between Cambridge and Ely. The clients are two academics, one an historian the other a philosopher, who have a young family. Built on the reduced levels of the fens, the existing house was refurbished and a double height reception room added. The new and old are linked by a library at first floor, new stair with tower study, kitchen and entrance. The frame of the new building was in balau hardwood and skinned in wide cedar boarding fixed with phosphor bronze bolts.

The double height walls were as a result only 170 mm thick. Some of the boarding was steam bent to the radiused gable.

C: N Zeeman and J Burt
SE: Peter Dann and Partners
MC: Coulson
A: EP, MM*, MP
Dates: 1988–1990

Playground
Porto Carras
Chalkidiki
Greece

Unbuilt proposal for play structures and a playground for children on holiday at the hotel complex of Porto Carras. The hotel mega structures designed like beached cruise liners were not conceived in terms of the archaic landscape in to which they had been thrust in the late 1960s. Our proposal was, in a small way, an attempt to mediate between the sea and the backdrop of olive tree stippled hills. Using play structures as primitive musical instruments and engaging the senses with colour, texture and scale.

A: EP, DB-C
Date: 1989

Office Building W3
Stockley Park
London

A design for a flexible office building in one of the best regarded business parks in Europe, masterplanned by Arup Associates near Heathrow, London. The north and south wings of the building are splayed to establish a sequential passage into the building, opening views across the lakeside and the surrounding landscape. Amongst several innovations is the first major UK application of pre-fabricated silicone bonded glass block panels. This created translucent walls, allowing light to penetrate deep into the office floor plate.

C: Stockley Park Consortium Ltd
PM: Schal
M&E / SE: Ove Arup and Partners
QS: Davis Langdon & Everest
A: EP, PM*, AM, AB, MM, AG, RK, NJ
Dates: 1989–1991

The Club Building
Chiswick Park
London

The site for the Club building was at the junction of the entrance avenue and the central space of Chiswick Park, a development of offices on the site of the former London Omnibus works. The Club building's larger neighbours were designed by architects Foster, Rogers, Ahrens Burton and Koraleck, Foggo and Farrell. Farrell and Co were with Hanna/Olin responsible for the site layout and landscape architecture. The Club included conference/marketing facilities and a brasserie that were adjacent to the arrival square. The larger volumes included a sports complex which contained an indoor six lane 25 metre swimming pool with rooftop tennis court, a gymnasium and squash courts. All of these were situated within a landscape as garden rooms adjacent to a storm water retention lake. The scheme came to a halt as a result of the construction recession in the 1990s.

C: Stanhope Trafalgor plc
PM: Trollope & Colls Mgt
M&E: Jaros Baum & Bolles Ltd
SE: Waterman Partnership
LA: Hanna/Olin Ltd
A: EP, RW, AB, NJ, RK, RM
Dates: 1989–1991

Market Rasen
Lincolnshire

Health Centre for local General Medical practice funded under a government cost rent scheme. A collonade to the Street and a double height waiting room affirm the building's public role. The waiting room is a discrete element and the surgery, examination and consulting rooms and administration form a rectangle to one side around a lantern-lit internal court.

C: Drs PEPT
SE: Peter Dann & Partners
MC: Coseley Contracts
A: EP, NG, ET* (AM, WM, GH, CG, MP)
Dates: 1989–1991

Rediscovering the Public Realm

Exhibition at the Heinz gallery in 1990 curated by *Blueprint*, as a response by five different practices including Branson Coates, Powell-Tuck Conner and Orefelt, Zaha Hadid and Allies and Morrison, to a perceived crisis in the design of the public realm. Our exhibit titled *The Space Between* concentrated on the literal and metaphoric qualities of the urban passage focusing on Brydge's Place between Trafalgar Square and The Strand. An installation of cabinets to house objects, information and to light the way drew on the poetics of surrealist literature to reach beyond the picturesque of the 1960s Civic Trust beautification movement. It was an attempt to rediscover the iconic power of the shared objects of the public realm. The thinking that started with this proposal led directly to the work in Southwark, Lambeth and other landscape urban schemes.

C: *Blueprint*/Heinz Gallery
A: EP, RW, CW, PM, SF
Date: 1990

Corpus Christi College Cambridge Graduate Accommodation

We won a competition to reorganise the college's post-graduate site on the western fringe of Cambridge in 1990. The scheme was given planning permission but has not proceeded as yet. The site based around the mature gardens and large nineteenth Century house had been revamped in the 1960s by Arup Associates who designed the precast exo-structured student building of that period. The college had since acquired a series of Edwardian houses to the north of the site. Our scheme proposed the creation of one large garden from those of the individual houses. This arrangement would allow the culmination of an existing avenue of mature lime trees. Three new houses, of a total of 35 rooms, were designed around an informal court at the southern edge of the new gardens. The urban model that this arrangement reflected was the Begerinage sisterhood of the Low Countries which is typically structured as a collection of houses set around a common open space. A new gallery and reception space, together with a caretaker's house, were also planned at the entrance of the site.

C: Corpus Christi College
M&E / SE: Ove Arup and Partners
QS: Davis Langdon & Everest
A: EP, AB, RK, NJ
Date: 1990

Pembroke College Cambridge Theatre

This was an intriguing and as yet unbuilt proposal combining issues of the ordering of the whole site as well as solving space requirements at the scale of a large room. One of the aspects noted critically in the Masterplan was the creeping homogeneity of landscape. This proposal would have helped to restore a balance by creating a hard landscaped court with a sunken entrance area. The top-lit room was carefully engineered to use natural ventilation for most of the year and was environmentally the forerunner of a number of other built projects.

C: The Master, Fellows and Scholars of Pembroke College, Cambridge
M&E / SE: Max Fordham and Harris & Sutner
QS: Davis Langdon & Everest
A: EP, PM
Dates: 1990–1991

Earl Place London

Remodelling of an entrance space and reception to an awkward development incorporating existing external steps. A glazed opening punctured by bronze aedicule behind which a double height polished plaster wall, diminished with the rising steps, to draw people into the reception space.

C: Appold Street Development Ltd
A: EP, NJ
Date: 1991

Lipton Residence London

We were asked to consider either renovation or new build. The latter was not possible because of freehold constraints, however some ideas from the new build proposed were developed in the Pembroke Lodge (completed 1998). The existing house was stripped around the core structure and rebuilt behind the characterless street facade. The dialogue with the interior designer, Chester Jones, who provided all the loose items, textiles and one-off light fittings, resulted in a positive tension between the architectural detail and the interior design and furnishings. This project established a principal that we try to follow—only one home at a time.

C: Sir Stuart and Lady Lipton
M&E / SE: Ove Arup and Partners
QS: Davis Langdon & Everest
MC: Bovis
A: EP, RK*, SW
Date: 1991

Old Wardour House
Wiltshire

Old Wardour House was built as the residence and office of the Bailiff of Wardour Estate in 1875 on the ruins of the fourteenth century castle outhouses which were partially destroyed during the Civil War. In the 1960s the house was bought and renovated by the Hughes family. In 1990 we designed the conversion of a pavilion known as the Summer House into a dwelling and a studio. In 1998 we submitted plans to extend the existing house. It is intended that the new rooms will capture light in spaces that mediate between the defined rooms of the house, the fragments of the ruins and the surrounding landscape.

C: Mr and Mrs Hughes
M&E: Max Fordham and Partners
A: 1990 – EP, AG. 1998 –2001 – EP, LN
Dates: 1990–ongoing

Masterplan
Norfolk & Norwich
General District Hospital

In 1992 we were joint winners of an international competition for the design of a masterplan for a new 2000 bed GDH. Subsequent to the competition the Private Financing Initiative (PFI) was introduced and taken up by the Health Trust and as a relatively small practice we were brushed aside. The scheme now built bears almost no resemblance to either the landscape 'idea' or that the parts of the development should be designed by different hands and minds to avoid the bland homogeneity that would otherwise result. The aim of our proposal was to create a positive precedent for a new generation of hospitals by creating a coherent setting of separate but interdependent buildings bound by a central landscape. The place of arrival embodied the civic role of the hospital. The entrance space is a square with out patients to the east and maternity and paediatric care to the west. The square faces principally into the landscape where the geriatric and mental hospitals are set to east and west respectively. The central parkland offers an environment of recuperation within the regenerative world of nature and into which all the wards of the hospital are directed. Thinking about this scale of making was important for later projects most obviously Granta Park.

M&E / SE: Ove Arup & Partners
Hospital Planning: Medical Planning Associates USA
Architectural Consultants: Peter Carl and Dalibor Vesely
LA: Cambridge Landscape Architects
A: EP, PM, CW, NJ, RK
Date: 1992

Fitzwilliam Museum
Cambridge

Invited competition entry for an extension to the north of the museum on a site next to the Peterhouse College Fellows Garden. Our proposal took the form of Baseris (the architect of the Fitzwilliam) proposed but unbuilt wing as a starting point to create new galleries, education and staff offices. The latter were positioned underground and naturally lit from light slots along the perimeter. The project was eventually doomed because of the neighbour's objections and lobbying of English Heritage.

C: The Syndics of the Fitzwilliam Museum
A: EP, RK, SW (model: NG)
Date: 1993

St George's Hall
Windsor Castle

Invited as one of ten teams to make sketch proposals for the rebuilding of St George's Hall after the fire of 1992 which had revealed elements of the plantagenet hall and chapel beneath Wyatvilles's cosmetic neo-Gothic decorations. Instead of replicating the rhythm of the window openings and blind aedicules the intention of our proposal was to create a wall of fictive panoramas by relocating Mantegna's *Triumphs of Caesar*, thought to have been originally housed in a long gallery lit from one side. They also currently poorly housed at Hampton Court. The architectural order would have then followed this idea with entrance to the Hall via low doorways under the paintings and the establishment of a series of new horizons culminating with the opening of the chapel to the room.

C: Her Majesty the Queen
A: EP, SW
Date: 1993

Sports Hall
Leytonstone School
London

Design of a sports hall sited in close proximity to a residential neighbourhood. The large rectangular building located between a hard and soft playground. Because of the change in level the building acts as a retention structure to the upper hard playground with a long wall forming a ball game backdrop. The roof to this side presents a continuous horizontal eave. Diaphragm walls supported the folded plate stress skin timber roof. An elegant solution, the scheme was developed to stage E with the local authority technical team before being shelved.

C: London Borough of Walthamstow
QS: Local Authority Technical Department
A: EP, SW
Date: 1993

Pembroke College
Cambridge
New Lodge and Student
Accommodation Building

The complex nature of this building in an urban context between town streets and a collegiate interior is illustrated by the 15 elevations that make up the exterior. The building is a single entity of several parts which are: the Master's Lodge, a family dwelling that can either absorb or shed bedrooms at the second floor whilst offering two large collegiate function rooms; a teaching fellows flat, two large common rooms; 92 student rooms; a modest car park and a basement with storage; computing; music and gym facilities.

C: The Masters, Fellows and Scholars of
Pembroke College
M&E / SE: Ove Arup and Partners
QS: Dearle and Henderson
MC: RG Carter
A: EP, PM*, SW*, EH, HT, HM, ABU, PK, JS, NJ, RK
Dates: 1993–1997

Ministry of Sound
London

Working for this organisation was difficult and unorthodox. It was five years old and had just celebrated its anniversary by bearing a logo and text message reading "Lasts longer than a Royal Marriage" onto Buckingham Palace. We were invited to design two bars, one at an upper level, the other in an arch of the railway viaduct within the framework of the existing club. One had to transform into a dance floor and DJ stand, the other into a chill out space after the alcohol licensing hours of 2am. The bar-bed was an artefact design, and coincided with another research project which culminated in *On Certain Possibilities* (BDP, 1999).

C: Ministry of Sound
A: EP, RK, SW
Date: 1994

The Ritz Hotel
Feasibility Study
London

Through our work in Kuala Lumpur we were introduced to the Mandarin Oriental Hotel Group. We then won a competition to refurbish the rooms, back of house, roof and the garden of the Ritz Hotel, Piccadilly. Six months of preparatory work on this once grand hotel where rooms and suites had been meanly refurbished in the late 1970s came to an abrupt end when the hotel was sold. Abortive work but the first introduction to: the hotel as a fascinating architectural genre; the Mandarin Group who were to return to London with the purchase of the Hyde Park Hotel; and to

the work of Charles Mews and Dawes whose original planning and detailing of what was the first steel framed building in London.

C: Trafalgar House
M&E / SE: Ove Arup and Partners
A: EP, NG, RK, JK
Date: 1994

Sussex Innovation Centre
Falmer

The Innovation Centre is intended to nurture new businesses in the fields of communications and physical science, by providing them with technological and managerial skills. The building includes offices, public areas, conference rooms and a cafe. The definition of the plan creates a new public space which in turn reciprocates definition of the building in a way that learns from the Hellenistic stoa. It also aligns with the Basil Spence masterplan for Sussex University which dictates an East–West orientation for the building.

C: Sussex Innovation Centre Development
M&E / SE: Ove Arup and Partners
QS: Franklin and Andrews
A: EP, PM, RK, NG, DK
Dates: 1994–1996

Offices
Tras Street
Singapore

The complete reconstruction of the shop house behind the listed facade called for the adaptation of the traditional arrangement to provide new offices for a travel agent, and a developer's headquarters. The scheme respects the order of the original structure whilst creating a light and open interior. The retained central stairwell, divided at first floor level with a new glass floor, is transformed into waiting area of the travel agent and provides a private garden space to the offices above. A new mezzanine was inserted into the roof space to create a meeting space for the developer, which can be opened up through a series of pivoting shutters.

C: HC Abaca
A: NJ*, NG, HT
Date: 1995

Offices
Stornaway House
London

When Granada Group relocated its headquarters from Soho to St James, we were approached by interior designer Chester Jones to collaborate on the fit-out of the new interiors. The nineteenth century house was rebuilt after war damage to provide office accommodation on seven floors. The cramped entrance and stair hall were rebuilt with a gently curved new hall and stair paved in Purbeck marble. The lower ground floor has three dining rooms and two fully equipped conference rooms. The executive suites are on the first floor with the new board room above opening onto a roof terrace. Throughout, the highest quality installations for catering and media were incorporated. The interiors and furniture were designed to mediate the scale of the period rooms whilst acknowledging the modern management of the company and re-hanging their impressive collection of twentieth century British Art.

C: Granada Group plc
PM and CC: Healey & Baker
Date: 1996

Bus Station 1
Walsall

Competition for the new bus station. The idea was to create a lightweight stretched fabric oval ring. Pavilions lead off this circuit and were placed amongst a grove of trees planted in the central garden landscape. At night the canopy would have created a giant lightfitting— the domestic at an urban scale.

M&E and SE: Ove Arup and Partners and Traffic Engineering.
A: EP, SW
Date: 1996

Damai Suria Apartments
Kuala Lumpur
Malaysia

When Chris Wong left the UK after completing his professional practice examination, we continued to work together. He introduced us to the client who was about to form a development company following the family's decision to move out of the timber trade. Damai Suria was the first of Dawntree's developments and our first building in the far east. Chris Wong set up C'Arch and Design with whom we continue to collaborate when circumstances allow.

Cl: Dawntree Properties
SE: Arup Jururunding Sdn Bhd
(in association with Ove Arup and Partners)
QS: David Langdon & Seah, Malaysia
A: EP, NJ, HT, RK, NG and C'Arch and Design (CW, WS, IWF, FF, CL)
Dates: 1996–1997

Granta Park Masterplan
South Cambridgeshire

The opportunity created by the unusual joint venture between a developer (MEPC) and a free holder (The Welding Institute) to create profit but also an income stream for the latter to enable the building of a much needed new research facility. The section 106 agreement with South Cambridgeshire has created a landscape framework within which a mix of biotechnology R & D and IT companies can be accommodated. The landscape detail was developed by the Munich based landscape architects Latz and Partner and followed a tour of European landscape schemes that revealed some very good examples of sustainable design. The research for the building element of the design guide, which was itself a part of the section 106 agreement, involved a number of case studies and a conference on the physical requirements of laboratory buildings. The park has been built out to the limit of 55,000 square metres much more rapidly than expected.

C: Granta Park
PM / QS: Glanville Projects
M&E: Max Fordham Associates
SE: Glanville Consultants
LA: Latz and Partner, Jo Morrison
A: EP, JS, JM, RB, JSY
Dates: 1996–1999

Agace Residence
London

One of a terrace of modest listed town houses in Islington. The lower ground floor has an independent flat that was turned into a family room with an open kitchen. The rear elevation followed the massing of the traditional extensions by excavating a lower court and a double height volume mediated between upper ground and lower ground levels of the house. A floating glass clad top lit shower and lavatory was suspended above the stair landing in lieu of the original brick volume.

C: Mr and Mrs Agace
SE: M Pereira
QS: Bill Short Associates
A: EP, PK*
Date: 1997

Royal Lancaster
London

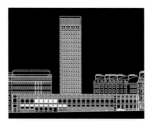

Competition for additional offices and conference rooms. Our proposal included the redesign of parts of the podium. The brief expanded after the competition to include most of the curtilage. The scheme received planning permission in 2000 and there is a possibility it may proceed.

C: The Landmark Group
A: EP, RK, SW, PF, PC
Date: 1997

Studios
Wimbledon School of Art
London

In 1997 we were chosen to design a new studio building to replace an existing single storey building that had been salvaged from site huts for the Festival of Britain. The gestation period had been lengthy because of problems with both HEFCE poor estates funding and obtaining planning permission. The building, now ready to proceed on site, consists of a 36 m x 12 m single storey structure roofed in 6 m monopitches allowing north light into the open plan. At the rear is a two storey block connected by a bridge at first floor to the existing building housing an experimental lecture / installation space above a canteen and common room.

C: Wimbledon School of Art
M&E: Michael Popper Associates
SE: Adams Kara Taylor
Experimental space consultants: Carr and Angier
A: EP, DK, JD
Dates: 1997–ongoing

Offices for Stanhope
London

This was our second office fit out for Stuart Lipton and his company which was smaller following the property slump of the early 1990s. More economical than the first project, colour and the abstraction of detail was used as a principle rather than materials. The refurbishment involved the reconfiguring of ground and first floor office space. The ground floor was treated as a landscape in which the primary colours of the piers are foreground to the background of muted greys and yellows. The first floor consisted of a central reception area surrounded by meeting rooms with partially glazed screens which give selective views onto the street.

C: Stanhope plc
M&E: JB & B
SE: Waterman Partnership
A: EP, IS*
Date: 1997

Taylor Residence
London

This project is a conversion of two existing maisonettes into a family house in Knightsbridge conservation area. The two parts of the building—a concrete-framed 30s structure and a nineteenth century mews house—are linked by a new four-storey stairwell and staircase covered by a glass roof, connecting to the roof terrace.

C: The Lady Helen and Mr Timothy Taylor
M&E: Michael Popper Associates
SE: Adams Kara Taylor
QS: Dearle & Henderson
A: EP, JS*, IS
Dates: 1997–1998

Southwark Gateway
London

New public space, tourist information centre, stone needle, interactive information wall, and hard landscaping. Following an open competition we were one of seven practices that were commissioned to develop ideas. Our proposal created a new public space as a gateway into the London Borough of Southwark. The tourist information centre is carved out of the tough urban condition adjacent to London Bridge and London Bridge Station. It is an insertion into a tight left over space that acts to enliven the surrounding historic area.

C: London Borough of Southwark
M&E: Michael Popper Associates
SE: Adams Kara Taylor
QS: Dearle & Henderson
A: EP, SW*, RB, JSY
Dates: 1997–1999

Mandarin Oriental Hotel
London

We undertook three phases of work: first phase included the replacement of all lifts, two new shafts, redevelopment of the ninth floor for rooms, the redesign of public spaces including the reception and public rooms (undertaken with Interior Design Consultants Alain Mertens and Chester Jones). The second phase included the architectural framework for floor by floor room improvements. The third phase, which had necessitated the closure of the hotel for six months, was focused on the two lower floors and included new kitchens, new staff facilities, new public amenities and the Spa.

C: Mandarin Oriental Hotel Group
A: phases 1 and 2: EP, RK*, DK, PF, RC
phase 3: EP, NJ*, LN, NL, MC, NM
Dates: 1997–2000

Fashion Store
Kings Road

Joanna Economakis is a well known member of London's fashion industry. Her shop Joanna's Tent on the King's Road has been on the current site for twenty five years, before which she traded from a market stall. The design, a collaboration with Chester Jones, was to reconfigure and resolve the relationship between the corner with its need both to attract and shelter and release the potential of a basement hidden from view. The solution was the creation of a platform on two levels connected by two wide steps for the floor and to treat the bounding walls as a neutral surface from which shelves would cantilever suggesting a sense of embodiment. The shelves acted both as shelves to support and as the hanging element for garments.

C: Joanna Economakis
A: EP*, RC, RB
Date: 1998

Westlakes Innovation
Centre
Cumbria

We won the competition for this building, part funded by English Partnerships in 1996 The building embraces and protects the parkland setting at the entrance to the expansion of an existing science park. To the west there are dramatic views to the sea whilst to the east lies a belt of mature trees. The 3000 m² building is naturally ventilated and provides flexible office and laboratory space for new business with conference and IT facilities for tenants, students and the public. The poor quality of detail and construction reflects a design and build procedure that effectively side-lined us.

C: Westlakes Science and Technology Park
M&E: Max Fordham and Partners
SE: Adams Kara Taylor
LA: Marina Adams
A: EP, RK*, JEM
Date: 1998

Royal Academy
London

The practice was short-listed to take part in a competition for the extension of the Royal Academy to incorporate the building in Burlington Gardens. The scheme outline demanded educational elements –including a large lecture theatre for public as well as school use, with a series of smaller seminar rooms as educational support spaces–gallery space, commercial space and a generous restaurant. The siting of the scheme generated many urban opportunities which were developed into an outline scheme. From the original shortlist we were one of two practices taken to a second stage but were in the end not appointed.

C: Royal Academy London
A: EP
Date: 1998

Granta Park
Amenity Building
South Cambridgeshire

The brief for the building included some start up office, offices for management of the park, a cafeteria restaurant, gymnasium and changing rooms for both the latter and for the cricket teams. Originally the Welding Institute were going to relocate their own dining facilities to the building, but when the parties could not agree suitable terms the restaurant element was reduced and the communal aspects of the building have been radically diminished. The building responds to its site.

C: Granta Park
PM / QS: Glanville Projects
M&E: Max Fordham Associates
SE: Glanville Consultants
LA: Latz and Partner, Jo Morrison
A: EP, NJ, PF*, SB, JD, EH
Dates: 1998–2000

Lambeth Gateway
London

We were invited by Enterprise plc and the Borough of Lambeth to prepare concept ideas and analysis for nine 'Gateway' sites to the borough. This resulted in a comprehensive report which was enthusiastically endorsed. Only one of the projects so far proceeded; Lambeth Bridge environs which included improvements to Albert Embankment and the hard landscape and mature tree planting to the roundabout and the southern side of Lambeth Bridge. Other sites included; Clapham Common and Old Town; Norwood West; Oval Island site; Brixton High Street; Tulse Hill and Herne Hill.

C: London Borough of Lambeth
SE: Oscar Faber
QS: Davis Langdon & Everest
MC: McNicholas plc
Other Consultants: Civic Trees, Granite Union
A: EP, SW*, JD, PC
Date: 1999

Mandarin Oriental Hotel
Spa
London

The Spa at the Mandarin London is embedded at the lowest levels of the existing ten storey building and is set between the massive brick walls that are the structure for the northeast quadrant of the hotel. The plan is dictated by the footprint of the heavily booked ballroom that is immediately above, overlooking Hyde Park. The Spa below is its opposite, a place made for the dreamer. Spaces for solitude and contemplation like for instance places of worship have in common this aspect of spatial boundary that allows the mind to vault the everyday to access immensity, the infinitive, and the imagination. Materiality was apart from space and light used to reflect this abstract but deeply resonant idea of recuperation. To our brief Stephen Cox was commissioned to make site specific sculpture; the Azumis to design furniture with Luke Hughes & Co and Isometrix to design the lighting.

C: Mandarin Oriental Hyde Park
PM / QS: Gardiner & Theobald
M&E: Cundall Johnson & Partners
SE: URS Thorburn Colquhoun
Spa Consultants: E'Spa
Lighting Consultant: Isometrix
Furniture Designers: Azum, Luke Hughes & Company
Sculptor: Stephen Cox
A: EP, NJ, LN*, MC
Date: 2000

London Bridge Environs
London

After completing the improvements to the three dimensionally knotty puzzle at the junction of Duke Street Hill, London Bridge, Borough High Street and Tooley Street, we were asked by Southwark Council to bid for the design of the hard landscaping running down Duke Street Hill to the junction in Tooley Street. This area was about to pick up the increased use resulting from the new Jubilee Line station at London Bridge. The transfer to buses meant waiting , people would meet and rest here and the idea of the flow of benches developed–the latter principally designed by SW. The junction of Duke Hill Street and Tooley Street is the start of one of the most important South Bank routes to the Tate and beyond. Here the passing of time is marked by the boundaries of the demolished Wharf buildings and the the trajectory of old London Bridge.

C: London Bridge Environs
SE: Adams Kara Taylor
QS: Dearle & Henderson
MC: T Loughman & Co Ltd
Lighting: Metro Lighting
Stone Consultants: Ketton Architectural Stone
A: EP, SW*, JSY
Dates: 1999–2001

Offices
30 Finsbury Square
London

We were approached, as were a number of other practices, for what was to become our largest project by Jones Lang LaSalle development team acting on behalf of Scottish Widows plc, who owned two buildings forming one half of the east side of the square. One was an unloved 1960s building the other a late 1920 locally listed and well detailed ex- bank. The potential tenant, Invesco, wanted a contemporary design for their headquarters and so the facade retention favoured by the conservation officer and English Heritage set the scene for an intense P.P.G15 case study. Previous architects had tried to replicate a distorted version of the 1920s facade, an approach that had been rejected. The proposal had to be good enough to defend itself against many different lobby groups and to survive an intense debate at the planning committee meeting.

C: Scottish Widows plc
PM: Jones Lang LaSalle
M&E: Hilson Moran
SE: Whitby Bird & Partners
QS: Gardiner & Theobald
A: EP, RK*, MC, HT
Dates: 1999–2002

Chronological list of projects and buildings. Initials, represent key team with * denoting those who were project architects with built projects.

EP   Eric Parry
b. 1952, BA hons Newcastle 1973, MARCA 1978
founded practice 1983

NG   Nello Gregori
b. 1961, BA hons PCL 1983, DipArch Cantab 1986
worked at EPA from 1986 – 1996
appointed Director in 1992

PM   Phil Meadowcroft
b. 1960, BA hons 1981, DipArch Cantab 1983
worked at EPA from 1989 –1997
appointed Director in 1992

RK   Robert Kennett
b. 1964, BA hons 1986, DipArch Cantab 1989
worked at EPA from 1989 to present
appointed Director in 1997

NJ   Nick Jackson
b. 1964, BA hons 1986, DipArch Cantab 1990
worked at EPA from 1990 – present
appointed Director in 1997

SW   Stephen Witherford
b. 1967, BA hons 1988, DipArch Cantab 1991
worked at EPA from 1992 – 2002
appointed Senior Architect in 1998

Architects
AB   Alice Brown
ABU   Amanda Bulman
AG   Ann Griffin
AM   Alberto Miceli
C'Arch (for Damai Suria)
CG   Clare Gerrard
CW   Chris Wong
DA   Darren Andrews
DBC   Daphne Becket Chary
DK   David Kahn
EH   Emma Huckett
ET   Edward Taylor
FF   Flora Foo
GH   Gavin Henderson
HM   Howard Meadowcroft
HT   Henry Teo
IS   Ioana Sandi
IWF   I Wen Foo
JD   Juliet Davis
JEM   José Esteves de Matos
JK   John Kennett
JM   Joseph Marinescu
JP   James Parry
JS   Jane Sanders
JSY   Justin Sayer
KS   Kate Spence

LG   Lisa Girling
LN   Lisa Ngan
MC   Merit Claussen
ML   Michael Lane
MM   Michael Mallinson
MP   Mark Power
NL   Nigel Lea
NM   Neil Mathews
OL   Oliver Lewis
PC   Philip Clark
PF   Peter Ferretto
PK   Paul Kember
RB   Rakesh Bhana
RC   Ros Cohen
RL   Rula Al Chorbachi
RM   Robert Morrison
RW   Robert Wood
SB   Sam Brougham
SF   Simon Farjadi
VE   Victoria Emmett
WM   William Mann
WS   Wilson Sng

Administrative Staff
Elaine Labram
Emily Foster
Gabriella Gullberg
Gill Morris
Jo Reeves
Pam Sanders
Sarah Powell
Sarah Rutter Jerome

Photo Credits

Cover. GD

Introduction

8.	HB
10.	CSP
12.	PC
16.	HB
20.	HB

Artists Studio

24.	DG
28.	Tom Phillips, Bertran de Born, Canto XXVII/3, Dante's Inferno Talfourd Press '83
29.	MC
30.	MC
31.	DG
32.	MC
33.	MC
35. x2	MC
36.	MC
37. x2	DG

Château de Paulin

38.	Nello Gregori
41.	EPA
43.	EPA
44.	EPA
46.	EPA
47. x2	Alberto Piovano
48.	EPA
51.	EPA

Stockley Park

52.	MC
55. x2	DG
57.	MC
59.	MC
60. x2	MC
61.	EPA
62.	EPA
65.	MC

Lipton Residence

66.	MC
71. x2	MC
72. x2	MC

Ministry of Sound

74.	NK
76.	NK
77.	DG

Sussex Innovation Centre

78.	PC
83.	PC
84.	PC
85. x2	PC

Pembroke

86.	PC
89.	PC
91.	PC
95. x2	PC
96. x2	PC
98.	PC
100.	The Bath Stone Group
101.	NK
102.	PC
103.	PC

Agace Residence

104.	PC
106.	PC
107.	PC

Damai Suria

108.	HB
116. x2	HB
117.	HB
118.	HB
120.	HB
121. x2	HB
122.	HB
123.	HB

Taylor Residence

124.	NK
127.	NK
129.	NK

Southwark

130.	HB
132. x2	EPA
133.	The Museum of London
135.	EPA
136.	DG
137.	DG
138. x2	CSP
139.	HB
141.	CSP
142.	CSP
143.	CSP

Granta Park

144.	PC
149.	Realistic Aerial Photographs
151.	PC
152.	DG
153.	PC
154.	PC

Mandarin Hotel Spa

156.	HB
160.	HB
164.	GD
167.	HB
168.	GD
171.	HB

Welsh Assembly

172.	AP
174.	AP
175. x3	AP
176.	AP
177. x2	AP

Finsbury Square

178.	AP
180.	GMJ
182.	Putler/Armiger
183. x2	Putler/Armiger
185.	AP
185.	AP
191.	HB

Photographers

Gautier Deblonde	GD
Hélène Binet	HB
Chris Steele Perkins	CSP
Peter Cook	PC
David Grandorge	DG
Martin Charles	MC
Nicholas Kane	NK
Andrew Putler	AP

Acknowledgements

Where an artificial line is drawn in the sand for good reason, like brevity, there remains a lot that relates to origins and process that has had to be jettisoned. While many of the projects not covered in detail are summarised at the back of the book, others, often thematic concerns, like competitions in territories such as healthcare, dwelling and the public realm, were omitted.

Of crucial importance to the development of the practice have been a number of people who whilst not part of the fields of engineering, art practice or product design (and therefore not included in the list of project credits) have nonetheless contributed through discussion, criticism and their own work. Among the many Dalibor Vesely and Peter Carl stand out. Wilfried Wang, Patrick Hodgkinson, Sandy Wilson, Ricky Burdett, Richard Sennett, Stuart Lipton, Mohsen Mostafavi, Helen Mallinson, David Leatherbarrow, Nick Bullock, Homa Farjadi, Katherine Shonfield, Carolyn Steel, Laura Illoniemi, Fred Manson, William Mann, David Williamson, Bill Grimstone, Peter Teo, Robert Tavernor, Peter Blundell-Jones and Jeremy Melvin have made important contributions.

We have needed the help of dispassionate advisors and in this regard particular thanks are due to James Buchanan and Elaine Labram, and for a growing transformation in administrative efficiency to Gabriella Gullberg.

In the production of the book most of the drawings have been made beautifully legible for publication by Julian Ogiwara, a task at times apparently without end. Jo Reeves has co-ordinated the publication.

Particular thanks to Duncan McCorquodale who has encouraged and enabled this publication and to Paul Khera for bringing it to life.

205

Colophon

First published © 2002
Second edition © 2011 Black Dog Publishing
Limited, UK, the architect and authors.
All rights reserved.

Black Dog Publishing Limited
10A Acton Street
London
WC1X 9NG

t.   +44 (0)207 713 5097
f.   +44 (0)207 713 8682
e.   info@blackdogonline.com

Designed at PKMB.

All opinions expressed within this publication
are those of the authors and not necessarily of
the publisher.

British Library Cataloguing-in-Publication Data.
A CIP record for this book is available from the
British Library.

ISBN 978 1 906155 62 9

No part of this publication may be reproduced,
stored in a retrieval system, or transmitted, in any
form or by any means, electronic, mechanical,
photocopying, recording, or otherwise, without
prior permission of Black Dog Publishing Limited.

Every effort has been made to trace the copyright
holders, but if any have been inadvertently
overlooked, the necessary arrangements will
be made at the first opportunity.

Black Dog Publishing Limited, London, UK,
is an environmentally responsible company.
Eric Parry Architects Volume 1 is printed on
FSC certified paper.

Printed in China by Everbest.

Also Available *Eric Parry Architects Volume 2*
ISBN: 978 1 906155 25 4

architecture art design
fashion history photography
theory and things

www.blackdogonline.com